The Kingdom Constitution

is

The Gospel of the Kingdom

The Rule of God

TRANSCRIBED

Sophia Calloway

THE KINGDOM CONSTITUTION
THE GOSPEL OF THE KINGDOM is THE RULE OF GOD
INTERNATIONAL Copyright © 2011

by WORLDWIND PUBLISHING & GENESIS ONE DIGITAL LLC

All rights reserved. No part of this book may be reproduced or transmitted in any form or by any means without written permission from the author or the publisher.

ISBN 0982648871 ISBN 13 9780982648872
Printed in USA

The Royal Decree

On behalf of HRH the Great "I AM" and HRH Jesus the Christ the Son of Man and

HRH the Holy Spirit of the Almighty God,

I declare to each of you, that you shall be made to fully function in the ordained steps that He has given unto you, so that you are able to fulfill your Divine assignment.

I declare that all works written in this book shall multiply and prosper you, even as your souls shall prosper and that His power shall effectively flow through you thus from this day forth.

Hear Ye, Hear Ye

Hear the Voice of His Royal Highnesses upon and throughout the domain of the earth.

Preface

We are living epistles.

Our lives are living letters and documents which are read by all who see. We are a message, a prophetic word from God, to all mankind.

We have one Father who bore and created us. We are His bride. We are His protégé as well as His friends. We are part of His family with our family tree extending from Him. We honor the Father of our family. We honor our heritage regardless of what nation or nationality we were born.

He has written on our hearts and sealed us, His heavenly documents, with His character. In obedience we have learned our true identity, for as we grew, we seen less of ourselves and more of Him. He validates and verifies Who He is to all mankind, but begins with ourselves. We have been sealed by His Holy Spirit, because of our right standing in His Sight.

We are His and through us, others know that He exists.

We are His people and we come to learn more about Him and to gain understanding in order to magnify His presence in all the earth.

Introduction

To understand where we come from and who we truly are, we must have a foundation from which we can build. This foundation comes from the One who created and formed us before we ever took our first breath on the earth.

We come from all walks of life and all types of dysfunction. We have endured various life experiences that have brought us to this point in history and life.

We are not here by accident. We were created on purpose, for a purpose. We are created to fulfill His will on the earth.

It's such a difficult notion to grasp, when we see the confusion going on in the world. It's a terrible thing to look out into society and see people not believing God and what He has created them to be.

As people in this world, we are lured, tempted and led into those things that are not of God. On a daily basis we fight the things that fight us. Through exhaustion, we stop fighting, by giving in to what the world dictates.

The harshness of reality that is magnified through all types of media, has penetrated even the youngest minds. These exaggerations breed an array of tendencies, causing them to live out a fantasy life, instead of a life of purpose and direction.

We see preachers in pulpits that dishonor their post. We see politicians bringing disgrace to their position and families that are being broken because there is nowhere to go and no one to lead them.

Trust is a term that is rarely embodied. The world is in chaos because we don't know who to believe and who to rely on.

Some churches have misrepresented Christ through not being an example of what they claim to preach. False prophets are everywhere. They thrive in our earthly governments, our churches and everyday life. There is a lack of truth and misrepresentation freely lives everywhere.

Where do we go from here? What do we have to do to turn this world around and make it a place where God said we could prosper?

With people losing their jobs, houses, family structures and governmental promises, where does one go?

We see all types of people voicing opinions, but it is rare to see people actually manifesting the solutions.

Though this may be a surprise to us, it certainly is no surprise to God. What we think is a setback is just a setup for God to bring His rule to this earth.

There can be no other way out, except it is God's way. Politicians don't have the answers, leaders and businesses don't have the answers and not even churches as a whole have the answers.

We now have to go back to square one and look at who we are and why we are.

We have to learn all over again by going back as if we were children. We have to relearn what has been disguised as Truth. We have to rethink what we have been doing. We have to develop new mindsets for the purpose of transformation. We have to stop listening to "other gospels" that we have been learning for so long.

Through the deterioration of society as well as the church, we know that the power of God is great, but we just don't see it everywhere like we should.

Apostles are to walk in signs, wonders and miracles, but to see these types, I personally have not witnessed. These wonders are not falling out or dancing in the Spirit. The Holy Spirit can do that Himself. These are actual real time events that through them will materialize.

Too often there are those who take a title as a means of power and authority. Misplaced authority in one's mind does not bring power, but it will bring destruction and condemnation.

The Lord says if we believe in Him, He will give us power to tread on serpents, heal the sick, and raise the dead. Where are they?

We don't even understand the words "believe in." Most think that those words are just a verbal statement of the acknowledgement of an idea. It's like saying, "Yes, I believe that's a tree." Just because you believe it's a tree doesn't mean you want it around you or you would dare want to look at it.

It is no wonder that the world is as it is.

There are so many religions, so many powers, principalities and a kingdom in this world and everyone is picking what they favor the most.

The scriptures have been taken out of context and they are being

There is no accountability in ruling places, so how can there be accountability for anyone under any of these ruler ships.

Thank goodness that God's Kingdom is within us. It suffers violence daily. It gets mocked, stabbed and left for dead on a daily basis. We as

God's people, house His Kingdom. Our bodies are individual temples where He resides.

Whenever we listen to Satan, we believe Him over God. When we do, the Kingdom suffers violence. We give Satan the opportunity to attack and crucify Him all over again; thus what we are agreement with, we become an active participant.

We do have hope however. God's Kingdom is like a rock and though whatever may come against it, it will stand. In order to maintain properly this temple that houses This Kingdom, we must violently or intensely take it back in order to guard what is rightfully ours.

This is warfare in the truest sense. When the Kingdom of God is fulfilled in you, devils will flee in your presence. There is nothing that can get to you that is not ordained by God. You can live the life that God intended for you to have.

The Word of God has been watered down and abused through the years. It has been misquoted, misused and misappropriated. His book has been used as a tabloid. People quote it out of context, thus turning it into gossip and hearsay.

As world members we have not been doing what God has intended. We are to be light bearers, kingdom carriers and glory fillers. But look at us!

How can we call ourselves worthy and sing praises to God, just because everyone else is doing it. How can we declare the things of God when we don't even know what they are? How can we walk in power when we don't have a clue how to use it?

One thing we know how to do however is be "hypocritical and churchy." How can we proclaim the kingdom of God, when we don't know what it is or how it operates? How can we say we hear God and operate in all kinds of offices, when we cut down fellow workers of God?

God has placed us in a race, but it's not a race to see what title or position we want to hold. It's not how many good deeds we do. God doesn't want what we can do for Him; He wants to know if we will do what He wants us to do, when He asks it.

God requires one acceptable sacrifice. It's not your tithe or your offering. It's not how many boxes of food you give to the poor. It's not how long you have been in the choir.

He wants YOU. He wants your mind, your body, your soul and your heart. He wants all of you.

Like Cain and Abel, Abel gave a more acceptable sacrifice. Abel's sacrifice was what God asked for and not what Cain was willing to give.

So here we are in this world and it is a mess. It's nice to know that God has not forgotten.

He had seen this before we were created, because it is written in His Holy Book.

He has not forsaken us. He said He would never leave us. He loves us so much that now He is willing to lower His Kingdom on earth.

In other words He is bringing the mind of the King down to an earthly level, where it is simple to hear and understand.

This Kingdom is the realm of God. It is the sphere of His Authority in all of heaven and earth. Within this Kingdom, we have rights, freedoms and responsibilities. We are given access and keys according to the level of our understanding.

Having seen Him in His Kingdom and out of operating in His Power, I can say that it is filled with glory and honor. It is pure, merciful and just. It is empowering and not condemning to all those who adhere to its constitution.

The constitution of the Kingdom is God and God is the constitution. It is His Rule and His authority that embodies it. To see Him, is to enter it.

Upon entry you gain access to a place in Him that He has reserved for you. Once you have entry, you will discover doors upon doors and doors that open upon your arrival.

There is nothing good that He will hold back from you. This Kingdom is like a bottomless treasure chest. It is like a seed that is planted that keeps getting bigger every day. It is like attaining joy that is inconceivable. Once you are in it, you would sell everything you have, just to get a glimpse of it.

No preacher can give it to you. No offering is big enough to buy it. You cannot bribe your way in. You cannot logically learn your way. No declaration will get you in.

The only One who has the key is Jesus. This key gives us access into His Kingdom power and authority. This key is the passport for heavenly citizenship in the Kingdom of Heaven. It is the key that opens the place that He has reserved for you.

So now it is my duty as a heavenly citizen to introduce you to what the Lord has to say.

The contents of this book are a path that will lead you into the "Gospel Truths" and will transport you into a deeper understanding of who you are and more importantly who Christ is.

I promise your mind's doors will open and YOU WILL SEE Him and identify Him in a way you have never seen before.

So welcome as I usher you into His Word and His Kingdom.

Chapter One

The Potter's Wheel

We envision being on the potter's wheel as He designs us perfectly for the destined task. He molds our form from the inside out, so that we will be able to hold what our Lord and Master has for us to carry.

Through the molding process, he cuts off the excesses and adds to our shape what is needed to strengthen our vessel. The more rigid we are the more we fight God's handiwork.

While we are in His hands we should cast out all notions of not being workable. This workable Spirit can also be known as a teachable Spirit, for through it we absorb the necessary water that allows our clay to be held together. This necessary work makes us pliable so that we when in perfect form will be able to withstand the heat of kiln.

Through submission we acknowledge who He is and through the bowing of our Spirit to Him, we surrender ourselves to the destiny He has ordained.

How special we are when we are chosen to be a good work in the Potter's Hands. He has already pre-choosed our shape, frame and design perfectly, in order to show us off to the world.

We are a commissioned work. We are individually His one of a kind piece. We are an original. We are His custom made lamps and are for display as well as functional.

As with any lamp the Potter always leaves room for a light to shine through. In this predestined determination He knew He already has a purpose in mind while we are still in the forming process.

The purpose of a lamp is to hold light which after all is the Lord's signature.

He is the "light of the world."

This special signature is engraved in us and its brightness is exerted for others to see.

This valuable signature on each piece is stamped with the Seal of Approval by our King and Father and His pen stroke is guided by the invisible motion of His Holy Spirit.

Our visible markings are seen by others. The very signature on our lives is written by the Lord Himself and demonstrated through the manifestation of our compliance.

The Lord is Alpha and Omega. The beginning and the end and He who began a good work is sure to complete it.

Just as at the beginning in the book of Genesis, we bear witness to His artistic endeavors and how everything He made was good. So we are also when he molds and shapes us into a new creature.

This new molding is the process of rebirth. This rebirth has draws parallels with our own physical birth when we first entered this world.

In the first stages of conception, God forms us physically in our mother's womb. We do not see the unseen hands that carefully construct and mold our eyes, nose, ears and hands. We cannot witness the millions of invisible cells that the Lord uses to build our brains and blood vessels. He alone knows the entire process of building our physical bodies. By His command we are pushed into the world through our earthly mothers. It is only after we are first born physically that we can enter into the rebirth process. This is where the Potter works on the spiritual forming or the second; level of our lives in order that we may become a whole being

Nine months of preparation; bring our physical bodies into this world through the water used in the birthing process. Now we begin regeneration again in order to be reborn in the Spirit.

Once reborn, you are birthed in Living Water, baptized as an adult using Jesus as our example, and then pushed out into the world to bring others to the light that lives in you

The compliance of the vessel and the potter thus become aligned and designed to do the work of what the Potter has designated

As we are molded we take on a new form, a new person is revealed. We are to be careful how we use this new form when we are trying to mold those under and around us towards the purposes of God. We should look for the flaws in other vessels for the only purpose of helping prevent further cracks that appear from the pressures of this world.

We must also remember that even though we can help others retain their shape; it is up to the Potter to do the work of rebuilding the vessel. Through this we pay close attention to the Potter Himself, in seeing that as He reshapes others, He also reshapes ourselves.

It is so important to know, that a potter can easily mold a piece of clay that is compliant with its former. The more compliant or obedient we are, the quicker the molding process.

When we come into agreement that the Lord's work in us is good, we begin to see the true revelation of who He is and we become a good work for Him to reveal to the world.

Why Are You Going Through This?

All this time you have been asking why this and why that, when the Lord only trying to show you a different part of Himself, while at the same time taught you a different aspect of your destined assignment.

This parallel revelation that you have learned allows you the growth needed in order for you to walk in destiny.

Your destiny simply is the walking out the true assignment of which the Lord created you for to begin with. Often people will ask, "What am I here for?"

Simply answered, "You are here to walk out God's purpose. You are here to do His will. Since you did not create yourself, how can you know yourself, except than to walk out how your Designer and Creator made you?

For example a manufacturer of a television knows exactly what that television can do. He knows that if the TV wanted to be a dishwasher, it would be impossible, for it wasn't designed that way. Therefore the manufacturer knew the limitations and boundaries of what He created. He knows what it's capable of and what its not. Just as our Designer and Creator made each one of us, He knows what we are made of and what His purpose for each of us is to fulfill. It's His plan, not ours.

In 2008 the Lord spoke to me and said "New Beginnings." In 2009 the Lord spoke It's a new era."

It's time to come out. It's time of the great call of the Lord our God to walk in purpose He has designed us for. In the words of our Lord "Thy kingdom come," we open up our hearts and submit ourselves to His call. We yield and look up to where our help comes from. In our heart's voice, we are in submission as we command with the Lord for His kingdom to come. We entreat Him to manifest his glory on earth. As we submit we not only ask, but open up our hearts to our Father with a loud voice and declare to Him, THY KINGDOM COME!"

Thus we entreat the Lord to hear our cry in order that we will be able to walk as He has purposed us to do. With hearts poised, we give up our spirit, the spirit of this world, in order for the Lord to use us to His full potential. Within this yielding, we are broken from every chain, every barrier and every evil thing that would dare come up against the Word of the Lord.

As our Lord hung on the cross He cried out to His Father and gave up His Spirit. He gave up His being so that His Father could raise Him up, therefore allowing His full glory to be seen and established. Jesus yielded to the Father even though every evil thing wanted to take Him over; but He trusted in His Father. He was poised in position for glory to take place. He made a decision to yield to the Father in the garden in Gethsemane. He aligned Himself perfectly and submitted.

Luke 22:41-43:

He walked away, about a stone's throw, and knelt down and prayed Father, if you are willing; please take this cup of suffering away from me. Yet I want your will to be done, not mine." Then an angel from heaven appeared and strengthened him.

Upon our knees, upon the threshing floor, we are allowed to be sifted as grain in order for the refining process to be established. Whatever the enemy sends, the Lord will use for His glory, so that we will be able to allow Him to live through us. Through this process the Lord shall intercede on our behalf as He did with Peter at Christ's death.

Luke 22:

Simon, Simon, Satan has asked to sift each of you like wheat but I have pleaded in prayer for you, Simon, that your faith should not fail. Again, we yell out at the top of our heart's voice. "THY WILL BE DONE";

We are now entering the time of complete submission for the Lord to kill off those things that need not be there. To kill off those things that are considered to be the tares in our lives, we decrease in our selfish lives, so that He can increase and be glorified through us. The coming together in Spirit as our lives reflects His. "ON EARTH AS IT IS IN HEAVEN'. Through this submission we fulfill God's purpose. It is then that we will see the glorious manifestation of our Lord. It is then that truly whatever we bind on earth shall be bound in heaven and whatever we loose on earth, shall be loosed in heaven.

Mathew 16:

And that's not all. You will have complete and free access to God's kingdom, keys to open any and every door: no more barriers between heaven and earth, earth and heaven. A yes on earth is yes in heaven and no on earth is "no" in heaven."

Our obedience and submission shall dictate the glorious manifestation we shall soon begin to see. Our alignment for assignment will have been completed. His will becomes our will, His mind becomes our mind, His wonders become our wonders. We are designed by His Will and His will alone. We become one with the Father. In being one together with Him, all things commanded in heaven are therefore reflected and commanded to come forth on earth.

Thus, the true knowledge of who you are is revealed through the Spirit of the living God. You enter into the realization of who you are and whose you are. This new sight comes from revelation and cannot be learned through books or counselors. It is knowledge only given by the Spirit of God, Himself.

Mathew 16:17-18

Jesus came back, "God bless you, Simon, son of Jonah! You didn't get that answer out of books or from teachers. My Father in heaven, God himself, let you in on this secret of who I really am. And now I'm going to tell you who you are, really are. You are Peter, a rock. This is the rock on which I will put together my church, a church so expansive with energy that not even the gates of hell will be able to keep it out.

The complete worship, adoration and fulfillment of the Lord, so that we can experience and see the true manifestation of God in our lives begins happening. Experience what the Lord has for you as you begin to walk in your destiny in perfect etiquette. The Lord's word cannot return void.

Therefore whoever has an ear let him hear what the Spirit is saying.

Preparing to Fulfill Purpose

All of our thoughts are known to God. He can understand what is in the mind of the Spirit, as the Spirit prays for God's people. We know that God is always at work for the good of everyone who loves Him. They are the ones God has chosen for His purpose, and He has always known whom His chosen ones would be. He had decided to let them become like his own Son, so that his Son would be the first of many children.

The Lord created each and every one of us, as a special creation of His own choosing. Through His fashioning, He gifted us with creative abilities that are demonstrated in many faceted ways. Though gifted with His thoughts and desires that have been imprinted on our minds and sewn within the fabric of our Spirit, He lovingly has given us the freedom and choice to use these in order to promote His Kingdom on earth. Each one of us is His own spectacular piece of art. There is not another that is like us individually. We should think of how special we are in that context alone. He knows we are so special, that once created; we were perfect in His sight, as far as our makeup and through our idiosyncrasies.

As He created, He lifted us up, smiled at His wonderful creation and placed it in a place where others are able to see His great work of art. He looks at us with thoughts expressed of how beautifully and wonderfully made you are.

He has established before us a path, with which He walks ahead, in order to prepare a way for us. His going forth sets a straightaway, clearing not only a pathway, but also while He walks in the lead, He clears the excess in front of us. He provides us with the necessities we need to walk out the pattern He has woven for our lives.

He has it all worked out.

"I know the plans I have for you." says **Jeremiah 29:11**

Our own specific designed plans are for each of His chosen people. We are set apart, perfectly crafted to do the mission and assignment that the Lord of Lords and King of Kings has commanded. We are special to Him. We are His own. His love is woven into every cell and fiber of our being. His breath flows through every airway that provides the life we need to fulfill His purpose.

Do not let anyone say that you are less than you are. Do not let anyone curse you, for you are God's creation, and yes everything He has made is good. When we walk in His purpose, we walk in the alignment or straight path that He has readied for transmission of purpose.

He has designed the people you were to encounter. He has designed the circumstances you needed to experience, in order for you to bring light to the individuals that He is now ready to put into your arena. Each consequence you have trialed through has brought you into a new light of Him and a new treasure of His revelation to you.

Since you are such a rare find, there is only one of you, which can go and do what He has called you to do. There is no one better equipped than you to do the job. When we do not walk in His purpose, we end up living through unnecessary frustrations and we battle with undesired enemies. We were not made to experience some of the events that have happened in our lives, for in those experiences, we were left defeated and depleted.

If only we would be in constant contact with our Teacher and Guide through every moment of our lives and include Him in our plans and courses of action, as well as our every moment thoughts, we would not have to learn such difficult lessons.

It amazes me however that even through these difficult trials, He loves us so much as to not leave us where we are, but rather picks us up and tries to retrain our minds once again. How special we must be for Him to be so intricately involved with each of us in our normal everyday lives. With a God so big and with all the sovereignty He holds, we cannot imagine or fathom how much He truly cares for each one of us.

We are specially chosen and set apart for His glory to shine through; if you were to step aside, how much do others see the glory of God within you? Do you have to do something for them to see it? Or do they see it, by just witnessing your walk with Him? It is said that you can tell how great the artist is by what He creates. Since God is God and filled with heavenly glory, how much of the glory of God, can others see in you as live as a living epistle for the Lord?

Mathew: 6:

"And when you pray, do not be like the hypocrites, for they love to pray standing in the synagogues and on the street corners to be seen by men. I tell you the truth; they have received their reward in full. But when you pray, go into your room, close the door and pray to your Father, who is unseen. Then your Father, who sees what is done in secret, will reward you. And when you pray, do not keep on babbling like pagans, for they think they will be heard because of their many words. Do not be like them, for your Father knows what you need before you ask him.

Once we understand that we are created and molded in the image of God, it is our reasonable service to build a relationship with Him. Keeping in mind that we are His and the fact that the Lord did not ask our opinion on how to make or create us, it only makes sense to ask Him for the direction in fulfilling our divine assignments. Through what I like to call wireless communication or in other words "prayer, study and meditation on His Word", we can comprehend His thoughts in the matters at hand.

And so, dear brothers and sisters, I plead with you to give your bodies to God because of all he has done for you. Let them be a living and holy sacrifice; the kind He will find acceptable. This is truly the way to worship him. Don't copy the behavior and customs of this world, but let God transform you into a new person by changing the way you think. Then you will learn to know God's will for you, which is good and pleasing and perfect.

We have discovered that our "design-ment" was intentional from the inside and out. It is our reasonable duty to ask or communicate what we are to do with how He designed us. In order to comprehend our task, we must come into relationship with our Father and follow the etiquette of what is acceptable behavior to the Lord our God. Upon doing so, we enter into His presence so that we can learn not only the assigned task at hand but also how to navigate through it in a manner that is pleasing to Him.

The Lord never creates waste and so as we come into the knowledge of Whose we are, we too appreciate the fact that our design, attributes and characteristics are a manifestation of His divine glory. We are the result of His spoken word. He, who created us, did so, so that He can glorify Himself back with the fulfillment of what He has purposed us to do.

The Lord did not create any two people alike on this planet. This fact alone should make us reflect on His creativity and awesome power. In order to tap into a sense of that understanding, we need quiet time in prayer accompanied with the walking out of scripture.

These variables enable doors to swing wide open, as the doors to our hearts are unlocked. We cannot understand our makeup if we don't take the time to get to know why our minds and bodies work the way they do. We cannot fulfill our assignments until we take the time to see what our task involves.

Just as with a cell phone, sometimes we get static when trying to communicate with the person. However with true assurance, we can take comfort in knowing that even though we may not always hear Him through the static of life, we know that He always hears us. Thus, the Holy Spirit intercedes on our behalf when we do not know how to pray.

In the same way, the Spirit helps us in our weakness. We do not know what we ought to pray for, but the Spirit himself intercedes for us with groans that words cannot express. And he who searches our hearts knows the mind of the Spirit, because the Spirit intercedes for the saints in accordance with God's will. And we know that in all things God works for the good of those who love him, who have been called according to his purpose.

We should take notice that God works all things for the good of those who are called to HIS purpose. We need to be reminded that we are designed for HIM. We are called according to HIS purpose. We should not prioritize what we think is our purpose. Instead we should be focusing what our life was created for or in other words His purpose.

The disconnection with our Creator will always have us confused in what we are to do. We will not have peace, until we begin to complete the Designer's assignment.

Our goal is to always have a secure connection with Him with no interference.

In order to achieve a direct line, we must acknowledge where the cell tower is or in this case "Where is the Lord's Stronghold."

Tuning into His frequency allows open communication with Him directly, while all the while angels tend to the airwaves so that His Word does not return void.

Wireless communication! Unseen words spoken on one end become reality on the other side. The manifestation of an audible voice comes through loud and clear in order to achieve the connection it is intended to have to begin with. Now taking that same technology and applying it in a heavenly way, here are the steps to having a clear connection. The Lord speaks through invisible lines and is heard through the Word and prayer. Upon receipt of "His Spoken Word", you are able to see the manifestation of what was said, as it is acknowledged and fulfilled through the person on the receiving line. Upon receipt, once faith is activated they are able to apply what they have heard. Upon the application of Divine instruction, they are able to complete the assignment that the Lord has laid aside for them "Wireless communication; God's communication."

It's free! It's limitless!
It lasts for a lifetime!
Don't ever leave home without it.

Code of Conduct

1 Peter 2:11-17 - I beg you, as those whom I love, to live in this world as strangers and "temporary residents", to keep clear of the desires of your lower natures, for they are always at war with your souls.

Your conduct among the surrounding peoples in your different countries should always be good and right, so that although they may in the usual way slander you as evil-doers yet when disasters come, they may glorify God when they see how well you conduct yourselves.

Obey every man-made authority for the Lord's sake - whether it is the emperor, as the supreme ruler, or the governors whom he has appointed to punish evil-doers and reward those who do good service. It is the will of God that you may thus silence the ill-informed criticisms of the foolish. As free men you should never use your freedom as an excuse for doing something that is wrong, for you are at all times the servants of God. You should have respect for every one; you should love our brotherhood, fear God and honor the King.

Kingdom Etiquette

Merriam-Webster defines it as "the conduct or procedure required by good breeding or prescribed by authority to be observed in social or official life."

In other words they are the rules governing socially acceptable behavior. They are the manners required in order to act in a characteristic or customary way.

Etiquette is a mode of procedure or way of acting. The word "manners" derives itself from the root word "manual."

Therefore in order to act in a manner that is authentic to the manual, etiquette is formed and performed. Through following the instructions and mirroring what is necessary to live an orderly life, we are transformed into living a life that is acceptable and respectable to our King and His government of which we represent.

Why do we need etiquette? The Lord requires it so that we will not only reflect His image, but also so that we can walk in truth because we are citizens of His holy nation. It is what is necessary in order to please Him, so that others may see His glory and image in us.

1 Thessalonians 2:12 NLV

"That you should live to please God. He is the One who chose you to come into His holy nation and to share His shining greatness."

NAS Version

"So that you would walk in a manner worthy of the God who calls you into His own kingdom of glory"

NLT Version

"We pleaded with you encouraged you and urged you to live lives in a way that God would consider worthy. For He called you to share in His kingdom and glory.

We must always remember who we are in God's eyes, as He watches us from His throne; His seat of authority and power.

1 Peter 2:9-11

"But you are a chosen people, a royal priesthood, a holy nation, a people belonging to God, that you may declare the praises of him who called you out of darkness into his wonderful light. Once you were not a people, but now you are the people of God; once you had not received mercy, but now you have received mercy. Dear friends, I urge you, as aliens and strangers in the world, to abstain from sinful desires, which war against your soul. Live such good lives among the pagans that, though they accuse you of doing wrong, they may see your good deeds and glorify God on the day he visits us."

Culture of the Kingdom Vs Culture of the World or Materialism

Definition of Culture- a: the integrated pattern of human knowledge, belief, and behavior that depends upon the capacity for learning and transmitting knowledge to succeeding generations **b:** the customary beliefs, social forms, and material traits of a racial, religious, or social group ; *also* : the characteristic features of everyday existence (as diversions or a way of life} shared by people in a place or time <popular *culture*> <southern *culture*> **c:** the set of shared attitudes, values, goals, and practices that characterizes an institution or organization <a corporate *culture* focused on the bottom line> **d:** the set of values, conventions, or social practices associated with a particular field, activity, or societal characteristic <studying the effect of computers on print *culture*> <changing the *culture* of materialism will take time.

Culture of Materialism

The culture of materialism is the process of buying things in order to fulfill an emptiness that lies within. It is the **theory that material things**

influence change: the anthropological theory that environment, resources, technology, and other material things are the major influences on cultural change

Kingdom of God Etiquette

What is included?

Manners

Manners are the customary mode of actions that one moves in.

Customs

The customs we follow is the usage or practice common to a particular place. They are the long established underwritten law.

It is the repeated practice and the whole body of usages, practices or conventions that regulate social life.

Fashion

Fashion is the method of artistic execution or mode of presentation. It is the form of something. It is the social standing or prominence especially as signalized by dress or conduct.

Style

Style is the social conduct or rules of conduct as shown in prevalent customs. It is the distinctive manner or custom of behaving or conducting oneself. It is a particular mode of living. The particular manner or technique, by which something is done, created or performed.

Behavior

It is the manner of conducting oneself. It includes the response of an individual to its environment. It is the way one behaves. Also it is the way something functions and operates.

Decorum

Is the dignity and sense of what is becoming or appropriate for a person of good breeding.

Propriety

This implies established conventions of morals and good taste.

Ambassador

Is an official envoy; *especially*: a diplomatic agent of the highest rank accredited to a foreign government or sovereign as the resident representative of his or her own government or sovereign or appointed for a special and often temporary diplomatic assignment

Kingdom

The realm of where there is royal power, kingship, dominion and rule. The realm is the domain including the subjects over which the king has jurisdiction.

In figurative terms it is the sphere of power or influence over the domain or empire. It is not to be confused with an actual kingdom, but rather the right or authority to rule over a territory subject to the rule of a king. It is the territory in which God's will is fulfilled.

What is included in God's territory?

Psalms 24:1

"The earth is the Lord's, and everything in it, the world, and all who live in it"

Kingdom of God

The kingdom of God is the rule or governmental reign of God. It is distinguished and set apart from all other kingdoms. It is the establishment of the work of God. It is God's manner or way of doing things.

Romans 14:17

"For the kingdom of God is not a matter of eating and drinking, but of righteousness, peace and joy in the Holy Spirit."

1 Corinthians 4:20

"For the kingdom of God is not a matter of talk but of power."

His ways are not our ways, therefore learning the culture and etiquette of His domain is imperative because of the fact that His kingdom is like nothing this earth can create on its own.

John 18:36 *"My kingdom is not of this world"*

People cannot build the kingdom of God, He has to do it. If He does not build it, how can we expand it? The only way is in the order of God. First, they can make the kingdom their priority and seek the Lord and His ways ahead of everything else.

Mathew: 6:31-33

"So don't worry and don't keep saying, 'What shall we eat, what shall we drink or what shall we wear?! That is what pagans are always looking for; your Heavenly Father knows that you need them all. Set your heart on the kingdom and his goodness, and all these things will come to you as a matter of course."

In other words seeking God's kingdom first is a priority. This verse in fact states the instructions we are to follow for the kingdom to come upon us. All customary rules and etiquette follow upon obedience to the instructions. These are accompanied by the desires of our hearts. Kingdom Etiquette is taken from the Manual (bible) which obtains the manners we are to apply. In applying the instructions we not only understand the etiquette, but we are also then able to apply and walk in the principles given. They thus then become second nature as we are changed and transformed by the Grace and of our Lord Jesus Christ.

Verses Emphasizing the Kingdom of God

It is a pearl of such value that they should sell everything else they have in order to be able to purchase it (**Matthew 13:44-46**).

Phillips Translation 13:44

"Again, the kingdom of Heaven is like some treasure which has been buried in a field. A man finds it and buries it again, and goes off overjoyed to sell all his possessions to buy himself that field. Or again, the kingdom of Heaven is like a merchant searching for fine pearls. When he has found a single pearl of great value, he goes and sells all his possessions and buys it."

Mark 1:14-15

1:14-15 - It was after John's arrest that Jesus came into Galilee, proclaiming the Gospel of God, saying, "The time has come at last - the kingdom of God has arrived. You must change your hearts and minds and believe the good news."

Third, they can pray for the rule of God to come soon: "Thy kingdom come" **(Matthew 6:10**; compare **1 Corinthians 16:22). *Finally, they can be ready when the kingdom does finally come* (Matthew 25:1-46)**.

The Lord's Prayer contains three requests, as follows:
"Hallowed be thy name. Thy kingdom come. Thy will be done on earth as it is in heaven" **(Matthew 6:9-10)**.

These three phrases mean just about the same thing, and they tell us a lot about the kingdom of God. "Hallowed be thy name" means: "Let Your name be hallowed, or honored"; or, "Bring all people to respect and reverence You.

" "Thy kingdom come" means: "Extend Your rule over human lives." "Thy will be done on earth as it is in heaven" means: "Extend Your rule over human lives here and now so that they will reverence and respect You." See Lord's Prayer.

Phillips Translation Lord's Prayer

Pray then like this - 'Our Heavenly Father, may your name be honored; May your kingdom come, and your will be done on earth as it is in heaven. Give us this day the bread we need, forgive us what we owe to you, as we have also forgiven those who owe anything to us. Keep us clear of temptation, and save us from evil'."

Special Things to Note and Remember

*In His preaching Jesus regularly invited people to enter the kingdom of God, that is, to open their lives to the ruling of God.

The Kingdom of God is made perfect when we partake in His image and become His reflection.

You pay attention to someone who is like you. You see yourself in them.

Obedience is part of relationship. The closer our relationship the more love for Him grows and the more obedient we become.

Culture Etiquette, Thoughts, Words, Actions
Thoughts-Acknowledging your Present Position

You cannot know where you are in life until you recognize your positioning. Just as God asked Adam in the Garden of Eden, "Where are you?" it is for our own good that we ask ourselves what the Lord is asking us.

Do you know where you are? At what place are you in life. In order to go forward with a sense of understanding we must acknowledge how our thoughts, words and actions align themselves with the ruling government of God. The first thing He wants us to do is to place our attention to whom created us in the first place. Being created in His image, He knows how we are designed and for the purposes we are to complete our heavenly assignment. We should not run from our God given assignment. Running from it will only impede everything that the Lord has for us. The Lord has His own Godly Positioning Strategies over this planet and everything and everyone in it. He can locate anyone at anytime to fulfill His will so that His will, will be done on earth as it is in heaven.

Just as Mary was a vessel to hold the governmental kingdom of God, so we are in doing the same. In changing our thoughts and minds to the way the Lord does things, we in turn become obedient as Mary and thereto become His vessel as we grow into the His image. Through our thoughts, words and actions we then become living epistles. It is then that others will not see us, but will see Him.

In order to become like Him we must follow the course set before us and acknowledge the commands that the Lord has put in place.

Seek Ye First the Kingdom Of God
Message Matthew 6: 30-34

"If God gives such attention to the appearance of wildflowers—most of which are never even seen—don't you think he'll attend to you, take pride in you, do his best for you? What I'm trying to do here is to get you to relax, to not be so preoccupied with getting, so you can respond to God's giving. People who don't know God and the way he works fuss over these things, but you know both God and how he works. Steep your life in God-reality, God-initiative, God-provisions. Don't worry about missing out. You'll find all your everyday human concerns will be met. 34"Give your entire attention to what God is doing right now, and don't get worked up about what may or may not happen tomorrow. God will help you deal with whatever hard things come up when the time comes.

Amplified 6: 33

But seek (aim at and strive after) first of all His kingdom and His righteousness (His way of doing and being right), and then all these things taken together will be given you besides.

Think on these things:

Philippians 4:8-9

Summing it all up, friends, I'd say you'll do best by filling your minds and meditating on things true, noble, reputable, authentic, compelling, gracious—the best, not the worst; the beautiful, not the ugly; things to praise, not things to curse. Put into practice what you learned from me, what you heard and saw and realized. Do that, and God, who makes everything work together, will work you into his most excellent harmonies."

1 Peter 2:11-12

[11-12]Friends, this world is not your home, so don't make yourselves cozy in it. Don't indulge your ego at the expense of your soul. Live an exemplary life among the natives so that your actions will refute their prejudices. Then they'll be won over to God's side and be there to join in the celebration when he arrives.

Why are you weak? Don't you see the strength inside of you? You are weak because you do not see the strength inside of you.

Decrees and Declarations Are Necessary
To Pull You Out Of Your State of Darkness

Philippians 4:6-7

"Don't fret or worry. Instead of worrying, pray. Let petitions and praises shape your worries into prayers, letting God know your concerns. Before you know it, a sense of God's wholeness, everything coming together for good, will come and settle you down. It's wonderful what happens when Christ displaces worry at the center of your life."

The King's Answers
His Royal Agenda

The bible is an instruction manual for all believing and non-believing peoples on earth as regarded in heaven.

2 Timothy 3:16

All Scripture is I given by inspiration of God, and is profitable for doctrine, for reproof, for correction, for instruction in righteousness, that the man of God may be complete, thoroughly equipped for every good work.

All scripture is to be spiritually discerned and is not to be understood through logical intelligence, for the Lord God Himself is Spirit and we must worship Him in Spirit and Truth (sincere, honest motivation to know the heart of God). The Lord also uses Wisdom instead of intelligence for He takes the foolish things of this world to confound the wise. 1 Corinthians 2:14; 1 Corinthians 1:27.

The Lord is Spirit; therefore He must be sought out in Spirit and Truth. This means that in order to understand the hidden mysteries in His Word we are to pray for His Holy Spirit and ask for His guidance to lead us into all truth. Resisting this entrance prayer, permits the spirit of carnality to offset our understanding and lead us into lies, confusion and misunderstanding.

For the carnal mind cannot understand spiritual things.

Romans 6:8

"For to be carnally minded is death, but to be spiritually minded is life and peace." Because the carnal mind is enmity against God; for it is

not subject to the law of God, nor indeed can be. So then, those who are in the flesh cannot please God.

Therefore to understand what He says in His Word and the fulfillment of it by praying for His guidance, we at the same time are putting Him first. It is reasonable to suggest that if we want to know something about what One is about, we should consult with Him directly.

Often there are those who in spite of themselves neglect to practice this exercise and inadvertently bow down to earthly things in order to gain knowledge of God. All the while God is waiting for you to search Him out so He can answer you directly. We end up looking for answers on this plane, when all truth is in His plane or seat of authority. Thus in doing so, these same individuals end up consulting with demonic spirits instead of the Lord, for their answers to heavenly things.

We should also keep in mind that Satan, the accuser and the deceiver, attacks those who operate in weaknesses instead of living in God's promises.

When we allow Satan to operate in our shortcomings, failures and mistakes, we actually give him the authority to penetrate all areas of our life.

Jesus made it quite clear to us, for He had to endure even more than we experience. In doing so, He gave and displayed His credibility of Whom and what He is. Jesus said:

John 10:

The thief does not come except to steal, and to kill, and to destroy. I have come that they may have life, and that they may have it more abundantly.

He also said Deuteronomy: *I call heaven and earth as witnesses today against you, that I have set before you life and death, blessing and cursing; therefore choose life, that both you and your descendants may live.*

Satan is clever and chooses the weak.

He especially chooses and attacks those of higher intelligence, for it is those who think, that they have more intellect than the One who created them. In essence when not obeying the principles that Lord has laid out, they exalt themselves and come into alignment with Satan instead of God.

He also preys on those who are self sacrificing or those who believe they please God by what they do, instead of pleasing Him with what God wants them to do.

Please note, these works are the works they place upon themselves and not the works that God has ordained them to experience.

This self sacrifice does NOT please God and results in self righteousness rather than accepting the Lord's righteousness.

Our righteousness is as filthy rags.

Isaiah 64:6

But we are all like an unclean thing, And all our righteousness's are like filthy rags; We all fade as a leaf, And our iniquities, like the wind, Have taken us away.

Our sacrifice that the Lord has not ordained therefore is a rejection of Jesus sacrifice on the cross.

When we reject His one and only and acceptable sacrifice, we come under Satan's rule and therefore he leads all into all the things that consist of misery, pain and death.

The only sacrifice God wants from us is the giving up of ourselves to do what is written in His manual. This sacrifice of giving over of ourselves in exchange of obedience to Him, puts us in a place of worship. It positions us in a place where we bow down to what He wishes for us. When we do not do apply revelation knowledge, we end up bowing down to Satan or to ourselves.

There is only one being who initiated the unsatisfied, complaining and in essence the non bowing down to God and His name is Lucifer. All those who defy the Lord's truth do this in spite of themselves.

Lucifer exalted himself against the Most High God and was cast down to this earth. Those who seek after his mind will have the fruit of it. Therefore, if the fruit of the Lord's Holy Spirit is love, peace and joy, then we know that if we do not possess these things we have the enemy's fruit which are death, confusion and defeat.

What controls our minds or rather whom we serve is displayed by how we search for the things of God, and is exhibited in the visible fruit that is manifested in our lives.

The choices are simple. If your life is in constant misery and distress, what are you doing that is delaying God's manifestation to bring you joy and peace?

Remember you are known by your fruit. Perhaps some of the best questions to ask are:

Who are you bowing down to through your actions and methods when dealing with people and scripture? What type of fruit is being manifested in your life right now and whose tree are you a branch of?

The Lord is truth, therefore it is impossible for Him to lie. We must accept His word through instruction of His Holy Spirit and those whom He Himself has appointed to give utterance to His Word.

If you receive information that is not confirmed by God's Spirit, then you sin against His Spirit by listening to the opinions and ideas of men.

Remember, the only sin not forgiven are sins against the Holy Spirit. Speaking against Him is also considered to be equal as not listening to Him.

Mathew 12:32

I tell you that any sinful thing you do or say can be forgiven. Even if you speak against the Son of Man you can be forgiven. But if you speak against the Holy Spirit, you can never be forgiven, either in this life or in the life to come.

Acts 7:51

You stubborn and hardheaded people! You are always fighting against the Holy Spirit, just as your ancestors did.

In closing, there is only one fear you should have and that is "the fear of the Lord," It is the; turning away from useless teachings and evil things. For the fear of the Lord is the beginning of understanding Let him who has an ear, hear what the Spirit is saying.

His Royal Agenda Part One
Hear Ye, Hear Ye!

**You Must Seek
The Kingdom of God First**

Seeking the Kingdom of God must come first in order to be able to access the throne room from where His rule and authority emits.

Mathew 6:33

*³³But seek first his **kingdom** and **his righteousness** and all these things will be **given** to you as well.*

We will now break down the word Kingdom so that you will have a clear understanding of what this biblical word means from the original Greek and Hebrew writings.

1. **Kingdom from the word** *Basileia* meaning -royal power, kingship, dominion, rule
    a. not to be confused with an actual kingdom but rather the right or authority to rule over a kingdom
    b. of the royal power of Jesus as the triumphant Messiah
    c. of the royal power and dignity conferred on Christians in the Messiah's kingdom
2. a kingdom, the territory subject to the rule of a king
3. used in the N.T. to refer to the reign of the Messiah

Basileia comes from the root Basileus meaning leader of the people, prince, commander, lord of the land, king

1. Basileus comes from the root Basis which means a stepping, walking
2. that with which one steps, the foot

Therefore seek the Lord your God and agree to walk in His dominion, rule and power. He will give you authority and rule over the dominion He has given you, when you are walking in His ways. This dominion is of Him.

Anything that the enemy has taken from us or is trying to take from us, God has given us the ability to gain that power in authority to retrieve it back. Since the earth is the Lord's and the fullness thereof, we have access to what the enemy has taken, and therefore hold our kingdom right to authorize and act in our kingly authority.

Righteousness comes from the root word **Dikaiosune** which means in a broad sense: the condition acceptable to God

The doctrine concerning the way in which man may attain a state approved of God.

It is the integrity, virtue, purity of life, rightness, correctness of thinking feeling, and acting and in a narrower sense, justice or the virtue which gives each his due.

Dikaisosune comes from the root word Dikaios which means righteous, observing divine laws such as His Constitution.

In a wide sense it means upright, righteous, and virtuous, of those who keep the commands of God. They are deemed innocent, faultless, and guiltless.

These are those whose way of thinking, feeling, and acting is wholly conformed to the will of God, and who therefore needs no rectification in the heart or life. They truly believe in Christ only. Therefore they are approved and or acceptable to God. They give evidence or proof of a thing by showing or teaching through what God has done in their lives.

Therefore you are to seek the Lord your God and agree to walk in His dominion, rule and power. When you do, you agree to the covenant of the cross and thus have received the sacrifice of Christ death for you. Now you can agree to be held blameless through His Son, faultless and guiltless and be used of Him. You can now agree to think, feel and act wholly conformed to His will and no need of rectification will be necessary in your heart or your life.

Do what is acceptable or approved of God in the way you act and the way you behave as you walk. When you do this it will show your faith in God and your lifestyle will resemble His. Others will be able to see it by how you walk and how you talk, the way you act and the way you present yourself.

That in itself will be evidence of what you believe and it will be a testament and proof that He exists, for your life will teach others without the use of words. He will give you authority and rule when you are walking in His ways and have mastered the control it takes to operate in His authority..

Added comes from the root word **Prostithemi** which means to put to, to add: i.e. to join to, gather with any company, the number of one's followers or companions he was gathered to his father's i.e. died

Once again, I must repeat: Therefore seek the Lord your God and agree to walk in His dominion, rule and power. Agree to be held blameless, faultless and guiltless and be used of Him. Agree to think, feel and act wholly conformed to His will and no need of rectification will be necessary in the heart or your life. Do what is acceptable or approved of God in the way you act and the way you behave as you walk. When you do this it will show your faith in God and your lifestyle will resemble His.

Others will be able to see it by how you walk and how you talk, the way you act and the way you present yourself. That in itself will be evidence of what you believe and it will be a testament and proof that He exists, for your life will teach others without the use of words, although your life will speak. He will give you authority and rule when you are walking in His ways.

Everything that you need in this world to enable your walk and the great rewards that will come as a result of your submission and behavior will indeed be joined or added to you.

The kingdom of God is the reign of God. It is the rule of God. It is the Sovereign God over us.

Who Am I?

The King's Answer

You Are My Will

Royal Agenda Part Two
Hear Ye, Hear Ye

I Am His Will
I Will Maintain My Focus

Phillipians 3

12-14I'm not saying that I have this all together, that I have it made. But I am well on my way, reaching out for Christ, who has so wondrously reached out for me. Friends, don't get me wrong: By no means do I count myself an expert in all of this, but I've got my eye on the goal, where God is beckoning us onward—to Jesus. I'm off and running, and I'm not turning back.

15-16So let's keep focused on that goal, those of us who want everything God has for us. If any of you have something else in mind, something less than total commitment, God will clear your blurred vision—you'll see it yet! Now that we're on the right track, let's stay on it.

Christ reached out for us before we even knew that He was there. As He outstretches His arm, He extends His hand first so that we are able to reach out for His.

Like someone who reaches down into a well to retrieve a drowning man, we can only hope to live upon the resurrection from the depths of what we once were in. We grasp onto Him in order to save our lives.

It is through Him, that we are only able to live. We are to show our thankfulness of the rescue by living as He would have us to do. We do this so that we do not fall back into the depths of where we once were.

With an outstretched arm He heaves us forward into purpose so that we can experience the destiny that we were designed to fulfill. With such force He pulls us out, that so much so, that we are heaved into a place of newness.

As we are pulled out of darkness, we focus on the strength that binds us to Himself. With such force we are propelled into an acceleration that can only be experienced by the power of whom He is.

We land on our feet running a race on a track that is designed specifically for our individual selves. Once we are aware of the track, we see the goal of destiny and the supernatural pull which forces us forward in order to attain our completed assignment.

We gaze and focus onward and we see the heat waves across the pavement that hinders our sight of the finish line. We strain our eyes to see the ribbon that is draped across the track that shows us when our race is over.

Since we cannot see the full end, we are comforted to know that He has designed the track and He knows how much oxygen we have in order for us to complete the predetermined steps.

We say to ourselves, "I know I can do this." And "I just have to keep pressing."

Though we cannot see everything about the final destination, we know we are on the right path, for His arm keeps reaching out for us to grasp. We are assured we are on the correct path, by the love and encouragement He gives us along the way. We know that He is there, for He supplies everything we need to complete the race. He is in charge of the destiny He has commissioned us to fulfill.

As we pass over each hurdle we are nourished by His body and blood. They provide our sustenance for the race.

We run faster and faster with each stride exercise a building momentum. With each leg stretched out to meet His, our focus remains not on our opponent but on what we need to do in order to complete the task. As we gain speed, He clears our vision enabling an easiness thus providing the necessary encouragement. With each spiritual cataract corrected, we are encouraged to run harder and are able to remain determined for what He will have us to do.

We repeat what He has told us. We remember what He has showed us.

He whispers to us each time we start to tire out. He gives us rest stations along the way, in order to provide shelter from the various obstacles that get thrown at us along the path.

We concentrate and utter His words to enforce what He has spoken in our lives. We do not take our focus off of what is most important. We do not look at others around us, for we know that just looking, will slow us down, and cause us to be distracted.

We sustain a sense of determination, so that we will be able to hear those words "Well done, my good and faithful servant."

The Holy Spirit, our coach who comforts and encourages us leads us on the straightaway so that we can be a testament and an example to others.

The way we run our race becomes the embodiment of hope for others on the sidelines who believe they are not able to do what the Kingdom is able to do. Our journey along the track provides an education and a knowledge that only the Spirit can display to others. His Spirit is living water and with every step our souls are quenched and drenched in His will.

Thus, each watering stop is necessary in order to walk and eventually run in purpose. It is those steps in purpose that connect us with our destiny. Without walking in purpose, we can in no way get to our destiny. We cannot win the race without Him. We cannot endure the race process without His Spirit.

We do not win the race because we are a terrific runner, but instead we are victorious because of whom we are running with.

What Are My Distractions?

The King's Answer
Do Not Be Mislead

Royal Agenda Part Three
Hear Ye, Hear Ye

I Will Not Be Mislead

Matthew 4
The Temptation of Jesus

Then Jesus was led by the Spirit into the desert to be tempted by the devil. ²After fasting forty days and forty nights, he was hungry. ³The tempter came to him and said, "If you are the Son of God, tell these stones to become bread."

⁴Jesus answered, "It is written: 'Man does not live on bread alone, but on every word that comes from the mouth of God.[a]*"*

⁵Then the devil took him to the holy city and had him stand on the highest point of the temple. ⁶"If you are the Son of God," he said, "throw yourself down. For it is written " He will command his angels concerning you, and they will lift you up in their hands, so that you will not strike your foot against a stone."

⁷Jesus answered him, "It is also written: 'Do not put the Lord your God to the test."

⁸Again, the devil took him to a very high mountain and showed him all the kingdoms of the world and their splendor. ⁹"All this I will give you," he said, "if you will bow down and worship me."

¹⁰Jesus said to him, "Away from me, Satan! For it is written: 'Worship the Lord your God, and serve him only.[d]*"*

"Then the devil left Him, and angels came and attended him.

In God's kingdom there is only One Sovereign Authority. Satan was allowed to tempt Jesus in the wilderness. Even though Satan is the devil, God used him for His divine purpose.

Just as we must walk in the purpose of God, Jesus had to as well, when He was led up into the wilderness to be tempted by Satan. When we study "led up" it literally means that God led Jesus to a higher place.

In order to have dominion in this higher place, He had to be emptied of the flesh and then filled through the power of the Holy Spirit.

The fascinating aspect of this event is that God was in total control of the entire situation. He knew that Jesus would pass the tests that were given, but moreover we should remember that when our faith is tested, we are to survive the conditions that Jesus illustrated through His actions. The tests were not for God to know whether or not Jesus was able to do it, because Jesus is God. More importantly, God allowed the tests so that Jesus could see how strong He (Jesus) was.

It was when He was hungry that the Spirit fed Him to the point that it literally flowed out of His mouth. The power of the tongue in speaking God's word is so strong that Satan himself cannot fight against it.

Therefore it is important for us to realize that we are the strongest, when we are the weakest. God will lead us into situations, so that we can further establish and speak the Word not only to our enemies but also to ourselves, so that in turn we are brought into the firmness of His Word. In doing so, we remove the hindrances of doubt. These occur when we rely entirely on other individuals to provide us the spiritual nourishment that we should be obtaining from God on our own.

For it is when we are filled with self doubt that we start hearing the words "what if" in our heads. This term Satan uses is a seductive lure to manipulate Gods plans for our lives. If Satan can get you to take your eyes off of Jesus, then he is able to place fear and doubt in your thought processes. This is then followed by enticing you with the place that he has for you in the kingdoms of the cultures of the world.

The only way we obtain self doubt is by doubting the One who created us in the first place. We hold a place of honor in our heavenly

Father's eyes. He is our King and we are His people. We are a royal priesthood and a holy nation under God the Almighty. If Satan can get you to either forget who you are or cause you to doubt who you are, then you are indeed setup to hold a seat in his earthly kingdom.

What is interesting is that the enemy seduces you with promises of things of which he does not have the power to ever own. When he tempted Jesus with the riches of the world, we must remember, that Jesus already owned it all. Therefore you must not submit your power to anyone but God. You must not give over anything that God says that you already own. This not only includes our will and our rightful place in His Majesty's service.

When the enemy tries to tempt you with anything that takes you away from your walk on His path, you must ask yourself, "What is he trying to take away from me that God says that I already have? You could also ask yourself what promises is Satan trying to give me, when his promises cannot be fulfilled. What everlasting gift can Satan give you that God cannot give you? What is Satan promising that will not last or will not come to fruition?

When Jesus was in the wilderness He was depleted of His energy and had had no food for forty days. He could not help but feel the emptiness inside of Him. It was then that the devil thought to use his trickery and deceit by playing upon the same emptiness that all of us feel at one time or another.

All of us are subject to go through stages of where a sense of depletion is evident. This depletion causes us to be self reflective thus causing our eyes to be on ourselves and not focused on Him.

Even though Jesus was depleted in the wilderness, it was the Spirit of God that brought Him through to not only speak, but also perform the things of God. Since Jesus showed strength, it is proper that we exhibit some of that same strength, so those who are our enemies can witness it as a testament to Whom we serve.

We are the saints of the Most High. We must believe, walk, talk and operate in the world in the same manner, so that others will be able to see what the Kingdom of God looks like. We must conquer the tactics of Satan, with the power of our mouths and the strength of our minds and bodies. We are powerful in the very fact that we belong to the Household of the Great I AM. We must make up our minds and decide whose side we are on and operate in the level of obedience that Jesus did.

It is God's intent to send us as His ambassadors to display who He is on this earth. We represent Him on this earth. We bring the good news of the Kingdom of God to all on the earth. Having said that, we need to reflect His image, not by doing good deeds on our own, but through the steadfast obedience in the call He has designated for us.

We do not need to recite scripture all day long, but if we have it written on our minds and hearts, the Spirit will do the rest by exercising it through our bodies for the world to see. We do not need scriptural manipulation and dissection in order to show others who we belong to.

When Jesus was led up to the pinnacle of the temple, Satan was trying to manipulate Him by using scripture to prove and advance his agenda. We must be careful not to use scripture to manipulate anyone around us to prove our point or to use as a sharp pointed instrument in order to get what we want. Using the word of God in order to prove that oneself is holy, is an unholy characteristic that God and does not reflect His image.

Often time's people use the Word as a sword to stab for selfish reasons. We also see also how the same word of God was used to inflict torment at Jesus arrest and persecution. Selfishness is a form of manipulation that cause plans to interfere with the strategies of God. When we use the Word as a manipulation tool we end up not only giving our Father a bad name, but we are not speaking His word in the manner that it should. In doing so, we end up like Satan by glorifying ourselves by undermining and causing turmoil in the true people of God around us. Consequently in the process we end up disgracing our Father in Heaven by displaying dishonorable behavior to others around us. We are not to cause others to fall into temptation.

Jesus was tempted three times in the wilderness. Peter was tempted three times before Jesus death. Jesus was successful in passing the faith test, by remembering His Father and applying His word. His focus did not leave His Father in heaven. Consequently the same Peter who had trouble keeping His eyes on Jesus, so He could walk on water is the same Peter who took His eyes off of Him once again at Jesus arrest. Whenever you take your eyes off of Him you will be lured and seduced and have the potential to lose all your strength.

Satan used lure and manipulation to try to get Jesus to throw down His life for him, by throwing Himself down off the pinnacle. It has dawned on me that Satan actually wanted Jesus to throw down His life, so that Jesus would end up serving him. Let me explain.

When you throw your life down for someone, you are honoring them with the highest honor that anyone could ever exhibit. If Jesus had done so, Satan could have held us ransom for all time. Where would we be if Jesus threw down His life for Satan and not for us or His Father? Also if you compromise by throwing your life down for anything that is not of God, then what are you actually worshipping? What short term decision do you make that could actually affect you for a lifetime?

Likewise we should never listen to the seductive wiles and manipulation that Satan uses to cast ourselves down. We are to lay our lives down for our Lord God and Savior.

John 15:12-14 (New Living Translation)

[12] This is my commandment: Love each other in the same way I have loved you. [13] There is no greater love than to lay down one's life for one's friends. [14] You are my friends if you do what I command.

There is no greater gift than a man lay his life down for his friend. If through the temptation Jesus would of laid His life out for Satan, then in essence we could of witnessed Satan as Jesus friend.

The manipulation used through what seems to be good and right by using and twisting God's own words to accomplish his own selfish needs, exhibits what to expect when we are placed in the same scenario. This event displays and provides what is a promised end to the use of these demonic tactics.

Jesus our friend wants us to lay our lives at His feet so that the same power of the Spirit that lifted and strengthened Him, will be able to do the same in us.

The Kingdom of God was given a preview of salvation and victory on that day in the wilderness. We are able to see the causes and effects of luring and manipulation. We also see that we have His power regardless of what circumstances we face as we are led up by His Spirit.

What we have seen as a test in faith in the wilderness, was actually a display of not only saving grace, but also a visual lesson on who we really are and how strong God sees us to be. Seduction and manipulation therefore are the elements Satan uses for us to gain access and a seat in his earthly kingdom. If Satan can change your position, he can affect your subsequent decisions. It is up to us to exercise who God says we are, in order to display the power, justice and majesty of the Lord our God and King.

What Do I Do About Those Who Hate Me?

The King's Answer
LOVE YOUR ENEMIES

Royal Agenda Part Five
Hear Ye, Hear Ye

I WILL LOVE MY ENEMIES

Luke 6

²⁷"But I tell you who hear me: Love your enemies, do good to those who hate you, ²⁸bless those who curse you, pray for those who mistreat you. ²⁹If someone strikes you on one cheek, turn to him the other also. If someone takes your cloak, do not stop him from taking your tunic. ³⁰Give to everyone who asks you, and if anyone takes what belongs to you, do not demand it back.

In a kingdom, the King allows you to encounter certain enemies to test your warfare skills. When He does this, you however never go out without the proper armor and support to accomplish your mission. The testing of your spiritual skills involves certain rules of engagement on how we are to address our enemy. Engaging them in the first place requires our practical theory being the word of God and our on the job training that ushers in a new type of strength that exhibits the glory of God. Each of us is responsible for how we handle each and every situation and the way we operate the God given strength that enables us to fulfill our divine assignment upon this earth.

Before we go any further we must examine what exactly is an enemy. Merriam-Webster states that the definition of an enemy is:

1: one that is **antagonistic** to another; *especially*: one seeking to injure, overthrow, or confound an opponent**2:** something harmful or deadly <alcohol was his greatest *enemy*>**3 a:** a military adversary **b:** a hostile unit or force

We are individuals in the Kingdom of God. Each one of us carries the Kingdom within us as we are houses or temples for the Holy Spirit to reside in. We must remember that Satan's kingdom is of the world and God's kingdom is not of this world. The role of the enemy is to overthrow the kingdom that you carry while you are on this earth.

When Jesus was born, He bore His Father's heavenly government on his shoulders. He carried this government on His shoulders, just as one would wear his cloak or covering. He wore it for the entire world to see. We also know that with each government we are aware of a military force that accompanies heads of state.

Isaiah 9:6 (Amplified Bible)

For to us a Child is born, to us a Son is given; and the government shall be upon His shoulder, and His name shall be called Wonderful Counselor, Mighty God, Everlasting Father [of Eternity], Prince of Peace.

Just as Jesus carried the government on His shoulders, we witness through His word how angels announced and accompanied Him upon His arrival, while Herod through the influence of Satan, strategized on how to defeat Him.

The promise that surrounded Jesus at this time is the same promise that we fulfill each time that we display the kingdom's government for the enemy to see.

We are armed not only with heavenly armor but we are promised that the Lord Himself will take care of our enemies.

The role of the enemy is to either kill or destroy the agenda that the Lord has set out for you to fulfill. He strikes in what appears to be "suddenly moments." He has a plan to discourage or distract you from the heavenly plan that has been set apart for you. His tactics are psychological and emotional. They are targeted to get you to move out of your position. If he can get you out of position, he can lead you away and distract you from the divine course that you are on. He will use harmful or spiritually deadly hits to get you down or cause you to rise up in the opposite ways that the Lord will have you act. You cannot fight someone who will not fight with you. The Lord goes ahead of us to make and prepare our way. Having said that, should you allow your focus to be on your enemies when the Lord is directing and leading the way?

Exodus 23:20-22 (New Living Translation)
A Promise of the LORD's Presence

[20] *"See, I am sending an angel before you to protect you on your journey and lead you safely to the place I have prepared for you.* [21] *Pay close attention to him, and obey his instructions. Do not rebel against him, for he is my representative, and he will not forgive your rebellion.* [22] *But if you are careful to obey him, following all my instructions, then I will be an enemy to your enemies, and I will oppose those who oppose you.*

Obedience is key when dealing with the enemy. Enemies are only allowed a certain degree of latitude when hurling the weapon which is formed against us. It is the Lord Himself who forges the weapon, so in essence boundaries are set in regards of how much we are to handle from whatever enemy attacks us.

Isaiah 54:16 (New International Version)

[16] *"See, it is I who created the blacksmith who fans the coals into flame and forges a weapon fit for its work. And it is I who have created the destroyer to work havoc;*

It is part of the perfect plan to perfect us into another stage of His Glory. When we understand that the enemy is there for our good purpose and when we actually apply what we are to do with them, we exercise a new level of faith and others witness the testimony that our actions bring forth.

Our King is sovereign. There is nothing in this universe that He does not see or have knowledge about. He is aware of every enemy and every plan of the enemy. Each foe or adversary that we have is under the influence of Satan, and the Lord allows their actions to draw a certain gifting out of us, so that He can display His kingdom way.

Our enemies actually strengthen us and enable us to display a different portion of the glory of God. How good He is to allow us to demonstrate how He looks at our enemy. We do not realize that each time we have an attack of the enemy, there is Someone watching to see how we are going to act towards each individual. The world waits to see, if we really have the love that it takes to address our enemies in the correct way.

When we understand that God is love, and that His Holy Spirit lives inside of us, then we come to the understanding that we are not only to love those around us, but we are to be examples of what it love looks like. After all God is love.

Matthew 5:43-45 (The Message)

43-47"You're familiar with the old written law, 'Love your friend,' and its unwritten companion, 'Hate your enemy.' I'm challenging that. I'm telling you to love your enemies. Let them bring out the best in you, not the worst. When someone gives you a hard time, respond with the energies of prayer, for then you are working out of your true selves, your God-created selves. This is what God does. He gives his best—the sun to warm and the rain to nourish—to everyone, regardless: the good and bad, the nice and nasty. If all you do is love the lovable, do you expect a bonus? Anybody can do that. If you simply say hello to those who greet you, do you expect a medal? Any run-of-the-mill sinner does that.

It takes courage and God given strength to not only fight your enemy but also defeat him. Whenever you are around an enemy, you are in a spiritual boxing ring and you are face to face with your opponent.

Your opponent comes in various forms and is dressed for battle. He not only has what he needs, but he wants what you have as well. When in the ring you are not to fight him, but give him everything He wants from you. The Holy Spirit wants to fight our battles for us, but we for the most part do not allow Him to take over the fight.

Taking it further, how often do we make the Holy Spirit our enemy, when we disobey His leading and His teaching? Through the consequences of disobedience, He ends up by our own perceptions being our enemy.

We are to treat our enemy by giving him all that he asks for. If he asks for our cloak, we are to give him also our tunic. God operates along those same lines as our enemy does in the ring. He requires everything from us. He wants our total submission of heart, mind, body and soul. When we fight or disobey, we in essence attack and become His enemy.

2 Corinthians 12:9 (Amplified Bible)

⁹But He said to me, My grace (My favor and loving-kindness and mercy) is enough for you [sufficient against any danger and enables you to bear the trouble manfully]; for My strength and power are made perfect (fulfilled and completed) and show themselves most effective in [your] weakness. Therefore, I will all the more gladly glory in my weaknesses and infirmities, that the strength and power of Christ (the Messiah) may rest (yes, may ᶠpitch a tent over and dwell) upon me!

Therefore we are not to fight the enemy or the Holy Spirit or even ourselves.

If we retaliate, we come under the same judgment that God initially held for our enemy to begin with. This is because the Lord said: "Vengeance is Mine." When we do nothing, we allow God to do everything. Consequently if we take it upon ourselves, we stand in the place of God, causing ourselves to be an idol. We then fall under the same judgment, because now we have become an enemy in addition to our enemies.

We are to let God take care of our enemies primarily because He has allowed them to be there in the first place. He does this in order that we may be able to exercise our power and choice that results in the obedience in faith of our Father.

Proverbs 25: 21, 22

If your enemy is hungry, give him food to eat; And if he is thirsty, give him water to drink; For you will heap burning coals on his head, And the L*ORD* will reward you

Ezekiel 24:11

[11] Then set the empty pot on the coals till it becomes hot and its copper glows so its impurities may be melted and its deposit burned away.

The purpose of hot coals is to have its embers consume filthiness. When you do good to your enemy, you are placing hot coals on their heads. God must consume the filthiness in their lives by your obedience in placing the coals there in the first place. The coals are the things that they require of you. When you give them, you actually love them by causing them to come face to face with God. Once they are face to face with Him, they cannot help but see themselves, for we are made in His image.

We cannot know who we are until we see what we are supposed to look like.

We must love our enemies just as Christ loved us. We must forgive them, because with proper perception, we come to understand that they really don't know what they are doing.

We are to love our neighbor as ourselves and we are to remember the golden rule.

Matthew 25:40 (King James Version)

⁴⁰*And the King shall answer and say unto them, Verily I say unto you, Inasmuch as ye have done it unto one of the least of these my brethren, ye have done it unto me.*

This includes our enemies because through disobedience and selfishness we not only make ourselves an enemy to others, but also make an enemy out of the Lord Himself.

One of the definitions of enemy is anyone who is antagonistic. An antagonistic person is someone who acts in opposition or incurs or provokes hostility. The purpose of someone who is antagonistic is to render another ineffective or to restrain and neutralize the power given to them to exercise. How many people do you know see you as an enemy? How often have you used manipulation to provoke another into hostility? How many enemies have YOU created? How many enemies do you think that the Lord has actually created for you to fight the good fight of faith? How much self perpetuated chaos's have you formed from your mouth and subsequent actions?

The Lord does not reside in chaos, He resides in peace. He provides us strength when we are weak. He said My peace I give to you, My peace I leave unto you. It is by the asking and acceptance of His grace that we can operate in a kingdom minded way. Through this grace He gives us the peace we require. One cannot have peace without the initial distribution of grace.

Both grace and peace are free, but they come with a price. That price is the giving over of everything that the Lord requires of us.

Loving our God, ourselves, and our enemies is an important part of kingdom protocol. Operating in God's expression is contained in the beatitudes. Mathew 5 shows us that the Lord understands what our true enemies are all about, while at the same time shows us the promises that He must fulfill.

Matthew 5

¹*Now when he saw the crowds, he went up on a mountainside and sat down. His disciples came to him, ²and he began to teach them saying: ³"Blessed are the poor in spirit, for theirs is the kingdom of heaven. ⁴Blessed are those who mourn, for they will be comforted. ⁵Blessed are the meek, for they will inherit the earth. ⁶Blessed are those who hunger and thirst for righteousness for they will be filled. ⁷Blessed are the merciful, for they will be shown mercy. ⁸Blessed are the pure in heart, for they will see God. ⁹Blessed are the peacemakers, for they will be called sons of God. ¹⁰Blessed are those who are persecuted because of righteousness, for theirs is the kingdom of heaven.*

¹¹"Blessed are you when people insult you, persecute you and falsely say all kinds of evil against you because of me. ¹²Rejoice and be glad, because great is your reward in heaven, for in the same way they persecuted the prophets who were before you.

Promises and unconditional love opens doors for those who otherwise would not be able to witness the glory and the kingdom of God. Through our every trial and sorrow, God knows who our enemies are and the promises He has in store. If we do what we are supposed to do, God extends His hand to handle our opposition in the loving way, He has set out in His word. We should come to the conclusion that if the Lord battles for us, who can be against us? We are to take that understanding and through His grace allow it to empower us with His peace. In doing so, God and ourselves defeat the enemy.

Questions to consider:
What makes an enemy an enemy?
Are they really an enemy or do they just not listen to you?
Is someone that you like to control (when they do not agree with you) an enemy? Did you know that you are someone's enemy? How would you like to be treated?

Why Do I Feel So Insecure?

The King's Answer
Esteem Others

Royal Agenda Part Six
Hear Ye, Hear Ye

**I Will Esteem Others
More Highly Than Myself**

Isaiah 66:1-2

This is what the LORD says: "Heaven is my throne, and the earth is my footstool. Where is the house you will build for me? Where will my resting place be? ² Has not my hand made all these things, and so they came into being?" declares the LORD. "This is the one I esteem: he who is humble and contrite in spirit, and trembles at my word.

You cannot hold anyone in high esteem unless you hold God and His leaders in high esteem first.

We are vessels which must be filled with the Holy Spirit and in order for others to be a witness of Him living on the inside of us. One of the most important things that we must do, is to hold others in higher esteem than ourselves.

We cannot do this however if we do not retain God in our physical vessels; the reason being, you cannot give what you do not have. In other words you cannot pour out what you do not hold.

The word esteem means:

- To regard highly or favorably; regard with respect or admiration: I esteem him for his honesty.
- To consider as of a certain value or of a certain type; regard: I esteem it worthless.
- Obsolete. to set a value on; appraise.
- Favorable opinion or judgment; respect or regard: to hold a person in esteem.
- Archaic. opinion or judgment; estimation; valuation

- Synonyms:
  1. honor, revere, respect. See APPRECIATE. 4. Favor, admiration, honor, reverence, veneration. See RESPECT.

You will find that as you grow closer to Him, your self esteem will grow.

Oddly enough our self esteem reflects our closeness, trust and confidence in the Lord Himself. When we truly believe who He is, and that He is our King and that we are part of His royal heritage, we come to an understanding that we deserve what the King wants for us, instead of what we want for us.

This permanent foundation provides a basis to build our relationship with Him. Our earthly assignment is too important for us to miss. The combination of life (the enemy and ourselves), combine to attempt to steer us away from our foundational esteem in the Lord. When we don't believe God and walk through Him as circumstances hit our existence, we will be subject to the following:

- Selfishness (not looking to God)-which leads to
- Pity which leads to
- Pity parties which is rooted in selfishness and unbelief which leads to
- Anger which leads to
- Either revenge (rebellion) and or depression (which focuses on you)

Like a dog chasing its tail we become entangled in our own mind, blaming God when God hasn't moved or done anything. The words that then come out of our mouths are then more apt to be accursed and in direct opposition to how we are to esteem Him.

Funny thing is, is that most live hypocritical lives and out of their mouths they speak a double minded confused language. They express to people in their life how much they love them, while as the same time are complaining to God how unhappy they are with their lives and who they are within themselves.

I have developed a new word for this type of selfish and low thinking behavior. The word is accursation instead of accusation.

Accursation is the saying that God is everything to you, and then out of the same mouth you curse those around you by not holding them in higher esteem than yourself.

Philippians 2:2-3 (New King James Version)

² fulfill my joy by being like-minded, having the same love, being of one accord, of one mind. ³ Let nothing be done through selfish ambition or conceit, but in lowliness of mind let each esteem others better than himself.

It is impossible to say that we love God, that we reflect His image, when we are not doing what He said to do, when we are first called to serve. If we cannot serve our fellow man, then it is ridiculous to think that we are serving God.

This high minded attitude will only move us into the things that are not God approved and thus eventually, God will give us over to our own defiled ways.

If we are depressed for extended long periods of time and when we have pity parties, exactly how much self esteem do we have? Where is God in our lives?

To all those who choose to cry over situations that God has allowed in your life, we must tell them to get over it and be the Word of God.

Be the word of God? What does that mean?

It means Read, Study and Perform.

God is looking at us on this worldly stage and looking at our performance. What He needs to see in us, is Himself. He needs to see parts of Himself working in the earthly domain. He needs to see if His Kingdom (His way of doing things) is advancing first in us and then in others. He wants to see if we are able to be examples of that Kingdom so that others understand how it works.

Here is an example. If you were to travel to a primitive country, you would encounter the natives of that land. If they did not speak your language, you would have to use signals and examples of what you are trying to communicate. If they couldn't understand, you would just show them how it is done in order that they would be able to do the same as you do.

Now if we take this method of active communication, we would sooner or later see others doing the same thing. This is one of the reasons that we are to be living epistles that others can read. We are then teaching a Kingdom language that others are not only able to see, but are able to relate.

Revelation comes from observation. The Kingdom of God is within you. If we believe He deposited His kingdom on the inside of us, then what we do is a testament to what we believe.

If we do not humble ourselves and serve one another, then we look like the world. If we speak the same language as the world, then with what selfish reason do you want to use God for?

When we operate on a worldly level and say we are His disciples, then we are making a mockery out of Jesus death, and therefore do not hold Him in the esteem that He ought to be held.

What is true SELF ESTEEM?

If the Holy Spirit is within our SELF, then where is the ESTEEM that belongs to Him? In other words if we hold God in such high regard and we say that He is worthy and that He is invaluable, that He is to be honored and revered, that He is to be appreciated, that He is to be favored, that He is to be respected, that He is to be loved.

AND

If He is all those things and He lives within us or within our SELVES, then He should not only be honored outwardly through our lives but also inwardly. Therefore anything that we say about ourselves must be of high ESTEEM.

The words we say must be those of value and worth. The same worth that we give Him, is the same worth that we must give ourselves. If we value ourselves then we will value other people. If we serve God, then we are able to serve others.

We should however not take the worlds definition of high self esteem. There is a fine line between confidence and arrogance; therefore we must remember that confidence boasts of the **Lord in you** and arrogance boasts of **world around you**.

True confidence can only come from Him alone. It is through this truth that we start to become aware of our true identity. It is He who has formed us and gave us the mind that He wishes for us to have. It is Him alone that sent us here to fulfill our heavenly assignment to accomplish destiny. It is only Him that has the blueprints that He has destined for our lives.

It is impossible to fulfill destiny without God's blueprint. It is impossible to serve God and others without the obedience to His Master plan. Being that He is our Master Architect, He knows how He formed us out of nothing. When we do not acknowledge and cooperate with the process, we travel out on our own, become our own God and serve ourselves.

Isaiah 29:15-16 (The Message)

[15-16]Doom to you! You pretend to have the inside track. You shut God out and work behind the scenes, plotting the future as if you knew everything, acting mysterious, never showing your hand. You have everything backward! You treat the potter as a lump of clay. Does a book say to its author, "He didn't write a word of me"? Does a meal say to the woman who cooked it, "She had nothing to do with this"?

When we serve our selfish desires, we serve ourselves and set ourselves up for depression. When no one honors the filth in our life we get angry. When we get angry, we become depressed when no one will enter in our pity party.

A pity party is a shrine we make to ourselves, where we become the idol.

If our pity party goes on long enough, we become depressed. We have placed the attention on our SELF and our ESTEEM is not worth anything. We must remember that if we want to make ourselves a god, then we better accept all the responsibilities that go with the position.

Also if this is all that you are filled with, then place close attention to what you are actually pouring into other people. A sack full of flour cannot pour out a barrel of water.

If you have true SELF ESTEEM however you are able to gladly place the same high worth you have in yourself into others. You will be able to compliment without double mindedness. Your speech will be consistent with God as well as everyone around you. You will have a flow of power and strength that others need to gain from you. You will have a deep appreciation of those who correct you in love; because you will know that this correcting comes from the Lord and not the world.

1 Thessalonians 5:12-14 (New King James Version)

12And we urge you, brethren, to recognize those who labor among you, and are over you in the Lord and admonish you, 13 and to esteem them very highly in love for their work's sake. Be at peace among yourselves. 14 Now we exhort you, brethren, warn those who are unruly, comfort the fainthearted, uphold the weak, be patient with all.

Holding others at a higher esteem than ourselves is a command from the Lord and we should treat it as so. This does not mean we are not to think highly of ourselves by expecting others to live up to our own expectations, but rather we should think of ourselves as servants to the Lord first, then to others.

Philippians 2:2-4 (Contemporary English Version)

²Now make me completely happy! Live in harmony by showing love for each other. Be united in what you think, as if you were only one person. ³Don't be jealous or proud, but be humble and consider others more important than yourselves. ⁴Care about them as much as you care about yourselves.

We live by example while at the same time demonstrate Kingly behavior. As we bow and give our lives to our King, we are able to serve one another. We are not to condemn or talk negatively about Him or the true leaders He has chosen for us to be under.

Exodus 22:28

²⁸ "Don't curse God; and don't damn your leaders.

We must remember that holding others in higher esteem than ourselves, has a boomerang effect. What we give out will come back to us. How do you feel when someone compliments you?

If we are in a selfish mindset, we must take into account how we would like to be treated. If the Lords name is operating in us, then we are of good reputation, because we take Him over anything the world has to offer. Our good reputation is the upholding of His High Esteem which is in us.

Proverbs 22:1-3 (New Living Translation)

¹ Choose a good reputation over great riches; being held in high esteem is better than silver or gold.

Our reputation precedes us. How many of us have a foundational good reputation? How many people have held you in high esteem? How many people have you held in high esteem?

Worldly people hold those who have gained riches in a worldly way in high esteem. They want what they have. Their desires are for material things and the flash of wealth that lasts a moment in time. Many in the church have preached the gospel of flash and dash. Grab what you can in whatever means you are able.

Their esteem is built on WHAT they have rather than on WHO they have. They pour their own esteem into others and thus lead others astray with their own version of worldly doctrine. They end up proud and un-teachable and blind to the ways of the Lord.

Kingdom ways are different. Kingdom people build their esteem in WHOM they serve. They pour Him into others and lead others into the same ways of the Lord. They are humble with great power. They are open to the ways of the Lord and have a teachable spirit.

Proverbs 18:10-12 (New King James Version)

[10] The name of the LORD is a strong tower; The righteous run to it and are safe. [11] The rich man's wealth is his strong city, And like a high wall in his own esteem. [12] Before destruction the heart of a man is haughty, And before honor is humility.

In His Kingdom we speak the same language and we do the same things as our King. The Lord is our strong tower, so we should not build one of our own as they did in Babel. Babel was man's way of getting close to God.

In unity, they spoke the same language or did the same things together, by building their esteem on what they are able to build for themselves. They erected pride as their statue of stature in life. Their pride is built on what they could do rather than what God can do.

They believed their riches and intelligence could get them to where they wanted to be and not where God wanted them to be.

They chose to do what they wanted instead of what God wanted. They were disobedient and went with the ways of the world instead of the all knowing power of God.

Genesis 11 (New International Version)
The Tower of Babel

¹ Now the whole world had one language and a common speech. ² As men moved eastward, they found a plain in Shinar and settled there.
³ They said to each other, "Come, let's make bricks and bake them thoroughly." They used brick instead of stone, and tar for mortar. ⁴ Then they said, "Come, let us build ourselves a city, with a tower that reaches to the heavens, so that we may make a name for ourselves and not be scattered over the face of the whole earth."
⁵ But the LORD came down to see the city and the tower that the men were building. ⁶ The LORD said, "If as one people speaking the same language they have begun to do this, then nothing they plan to do will be impossible for them. ⁷ Come, let us go down and confuse their language so they will not understand each other."
⁸ So the LORD scattered them from there over all the earth, and they stopped building the city. ⁹ That is why it was called Babel —because there the LORD confused the language of the whole world. From there the LORD scattered them over the face of the whole earth.

They chose brick instead of stone, because brick was manmade. They built on their own ability and did not build on or with the stone or rock. In agreement they baked their bricks thoroughly. In agreement they cemented the tower with the blackness of tar. In agreement, they built a man made tower put together by darkness.

Of course, the Lord knows the power of agreement. In accordance we are to observe the power of agreement when it comes to esteem. If we agree with the Lord in His Esteem, He will agree with Himself in ours. If we agree with Him in ours, then we are able to esteem others naturally as well as in a powerful way.

There really is no other way than God's way of exhibiting His esteem in us. The people in Babel's time held God's esteem lightly. Destruction followed because of their actions and belief system.

The Father, Son and Holy Spirit went down to Babel to establish what had already been done. Satan is the author of confusion. God just used His word to establish what had already been taking place. They stopped building a tower for themselves by the grace of Godhead; the spiritual authority that governs all. Why is this grace? Because they actually stopped them from further defiling themselves.

With this understanding, it is up to us to submit to that Sovereign Authority. It is up to us to house a place for His Esteem to reside so that others may partake of it.

Isaiah 66:1-3

[1] *This is what the LORD says: "Heaven is my throne, and the earth is my footstool. Where is the house you will build for me? Where will my resting place be?[2] Has not my hand made all these things, and so they came into being?" declares the LORD." This is the one I esteem: he who is humble and contrite in spirit, and trembles at my word.*

With the flow of God, we speak the same language. With the same language we are powerful. If we are speaking forth the same language into others, we will see the manifestation of God not only in others, but also in ourselves.

We are full of His Esteem. It is only right that we acknowledge Him in others.

Where Do I Look?

The King's Answer
Do Not Look Back

Royal Agenda Part 7
Hear Ye, Hear Ye

I WILL NOT LOOK BACK

Philippians 3:13 (New American Standard Bible)

[13]Brethren, I do not regard myself as having laid hold of it yet; but one thing I do: forgetting what lies behind and reaching forward to what lies ahead,

Mathew 24: 28-37

[28]When Lot lived, people were also eating and drinking. They were buying, selling, planting, and building. [29]But on the very day Lot left Sodom, fiery flames poured down from the sky and killed everyone. [30]The same will happen on the day when the Son of Man appears. [31]At that time no one on a rooftop should go down into the house to get anything. No one in a field should go back to the house for anything. [32]Remember what happened to Lot's wife. [33]People who try to save their lives will lose them, and those who lose their lives will save them. [34]On that night two people will be sleeping in the same bed, but only one will be taken. The other will be left. [35-36]Two women will be together grinding wheat, but only one will be taken. The other will be left. [37]Then Jesus' disciples spoke up, "But where will this happen, Lord?" Jesus said, "Where there is a corpse, there will always be buzzards."

17:26 [10] And as it was in the days of Noe, so shall it be also in the days of the Son of man.

The world will be taken by surprise with the sudden judgment of God, and therefore the faithful ought to continually watch.

17:31 [11] In that day, he which shall be upon the housetop, and his stuff in the house, let him not come down to take it away: and he that is in the field, let him likewise not return back.

We must pay careful attention that neither distrust nor the enticements of this world, nor any consideration of friendship that hinders us in the least way.

17:37 *[12] And they answered and said unto him, Where, Lord? And he said unto them, Wheresoever the body [is], thither will the eagles be gathered together.*

A judgment is taking place upon the earth. This judgment is for the reasons of separating those from spiritual Sodom and Gomorrah and those for the Kingdom of God. The Lord has sent His angel and she is crying out:

Revelation 14:6-8 (New International Version)

[6]Then I saw another angel flying in midair, and he had the eternal gospel to proclaim to those who live on the earth—to every nation, tribe, language and people. [7]He said in a loud voice, "Fear God and give him glory, because the hour of his judgment has come. Worship him who made the heavens, the earth, the sea and the springs of water."
[8]A second angel followed and said, "Fallen! Fallen is Babylon the Great, which made all the nations drink the maddening wine of her adulteries."

Characteristics of Sodom and Gomorrah and Babylon

1 Corinthians 6:9-10

[9] Don't you realize that those who do wrong will not inherit the Kingdom of God? Don't fool yourselves. Those who indulge in sexual sin, or who worship idols, or commit adultery, or are male prostitutes, or practice homosexuality, [10] or are thieves, or greedy people, or drunkards, or are abusive, or cheat people—none of these will inherit the Kingdom of God.

What Really Makes People Unclean
(Matthew 15.10-20)

¹⁴Jesus called the crowd together again and said, "Pay attention and try to understand what I mean. ¹⁵⁻¹⁶The food that you put into your mouth doesn't make you unclean and unfit to worship God. The bad words that come out of your mouth are what make you unclean." [e]

¹⁷After Jesus and his disciples had left the crowd and had gone into the house, they asked him what these sayings meant. ¹⁸He answered, "Don't you know what I am talking about by now? You surely know that the food you put into your mouth cannot make you unclean. ¹⁹It doesn't go into your heart, but into your stomach, and then out of your body." By saying this, Jesus meant that all foods were fit to eat.

²⁰Then Jesus said:

What comes from your heart is what makes you unclean. ²¹Out of your heart come evil thoughts, vulgar deeds, stealing, murder, ²²unfaithfulness in marriage, greed, meanness, deceit, indecency, envy, insults, pride, and foolishness. ²³All of these come from your heart, and they are what make you unfit to worship God.

True worship is the obedience to God and His commands. It is a lifestyle. It is not exclusively something that you do in church when you sing, pray, dance or run. Worship is the giving over of oneself in order to fulfill His purpose on this earth. We work for Him. He doesn't work for us, He works in us.

The Understanding

This is spiritual Sodom and Gomorrah and Babylon.

Just as Sodom and Gomorrah had to fall, so did Babylon. Each of these two cities had to be destroyed by the fierce wrath of God. We are in the revelation time of judgment. We are to make a decision and not turn back from it. We are to stay focused on the task at hand as each day progresses into another. We maintain a forward direction and do not look back to the things that we once were and the things we entertained when we did not accept the gift of Jesus dying on the cross. It is only through the acceptance of His gift that we are able to turn from our ways, and when we get weak and fall, we are assured that He is there to push us to His Holy place that He has prepared for us.

Exercise Your Faith and Confidence

Luke 9:62 (New International Version)

⁶²Jesus replied, "No one who puts his hand to the plow and looks back is fit for service in the kingdom of God."

We must know where we are in Christ in order to know where our positioning is in the present assignment that He has given. When we are called to HIS purpose, we are stationed in a new place. A worldly or Babylonian view causes us to want to look back at all the things we are leaving behind, which may include family, things and friends.

Looking back only sets us up to look at the following things:

- Regret whether good or bad
- Desires whether from God or not
- Remembrances that cause hindrance
- Makes us want to keep some things that are not good for us
- Sets us up to not walk forward
- Promotes what "I" would still like to have
- Initiates backwards thinking
- It stops us from working on the purpose that God has for us

Jesus said that whoever looks back is not fit for service in the Kingdom of God. How can we serve if we have our own agenda which immediately begins with disobedience? How can we be in obedience to God, when we turn away from the instructions that are set before us?

When Lot's wife turned and looked back, she in essence was turning her head and her mind away from the leadership in front of her. In this case she disobeyed a direct command from a heaven sent angel who had revealed Himself to guide and lead her way.

In those days, the angel was trying to save them from what God was about to do in the area of where they lived. He was not pleased with their behavior and how disrespectful they were to the Lord their God.

God spoke to Lot and his wife so that they would be saved from the sin that was so prevalent. He also wanted to save them from the impending destruction He was about to send upon the city.

They were told to go to the mountain for safety. The mountain was the symbolic place where the Rock would provide what they needed for shelter and safety from the impending destruction.

Looking forward to the Rock along with specific instructions, we are given the ability to live in the comfort of Christ alone. In a sense we give up what we want in place for what God would want for us instead.

In His protective mercy, He sends an angel in front of us to guide us and we are not to be disobedient for His name is in him.

In the same sense how many of us turn away when God reveals Himself through His word or instruction? I urge you do not look back. You will be distracted from your future if you look back. When He sends an angel to direct you, do not be disobedient. That angel has specific instructions so that you will be able to avoid the schemes and plans that the enemy has to entice you with. If you look back you will not be able to see the things that can corrupt your future vision. Not looking back will then be the operation of the faith that He has given you that encourages your perceived destiny.

It is by faith that we trust whom God sends to direct our paths in order to fulfill our given tasks. There is not one of us on this earth, who does not need help in doing so, thus by accepting this help, we are giving in the way that Lord commanded.

Our lack of belief will cause us to look back and in effect disobey what the Lord instructs. It is impossible to be righteous if you do not live by faith. Faith is the spiritual muscle that must be exercised so that others may be a witness of the unseen God in your life. Through what you do and the perseverance you exercise, others will witness who God really is in your life, instead of the lip service that most give.

When faced with opposition, shrinking back only sets us up to have someone set us up to be a slave instead of a servant.

Hebrews 10: 25-39

So do not throw away your confidence; it will be richly rewarded. ³⁶You need to persevere so that when you have done the will of God, you will receive what he has promised. ³⁷For in just a very little while, "He who is coming will come and will not delay. ³⁸But my righteous one[f] will live by faith. And if he shrinks back, I will not be pleased with him."[g] ³⁹But we are not of those who shrink back and are destroyed, but of those who believe and are saved.

Our belief and trust in Christ enables us to exercise our full rights under His divine authority. He has given us discernment through our spiritual eyes. He has given us leaders to provide us what is necessary to guard our path. He has given us a measure of faith that we are to exercise in order to manifest His working power within us.

Our level of trust in Him is compared to our level of obedience to Him. When we are given commands through His word, whether they are delivered through reading His word or whether they are given through the angel of the house or the prophets of God; He looks intently to observe our faithfulness to the instruction which is given. He looks to see whether or not His instructions on His righteous living are being taken to heart or if we delay in performing what He has commanded.

He wants to see if we are like Lot's wife when she turned back. Her lack of obedience turned her into a pillar of salt.

Why a pillar of salt? In disobedience she in a sense made herself her own god, by enabling her own command on herself and placing it ahead of God's command.

She placed her thoughts in front of God's thoughts, thus making herself into an idol.

Salt is used as flavoring and is used to season. Salt in the desert dries up moisture. In turning into salt, she in disobedience took on its characteristics.

The Spirit of living water was dried up within her and her life was in distaste. Her actions were not able to provide the divine seasoning used for strengthen the flavor of those around her. She was turned into a pillar which is a monument and a remembrance for others to see. She turned into a useless idol, the very thing that her thoughts and actions caused her to be. She served as a testament of what happens spiritually to us when we look back.

Anything that contains too much salt will cause us to die and dehydrate. When we are dehydrated we lack water. When we lack living water our life soon will come to end, just as the case with Lot's wife.

In a spiritual sense if we lack living water or when we don't want to take the instructional water given to us, we die parched and lifeless. We are useless to anything that the Lord will have us do.

We are to scatter ourselves throughout the earth in order to preach the gospel of the Kingdom throughout the world. Jesus said we are the salt of the earth. Salt is shaken and used to season those stale lifestyles of those not in the Kingdom of God.

Matthew 5:13-15 (Amplified Bible)

[13]You are the salt of the earth, but if salt has lost its taste (its strength, its quality), how can its saltiness be restored? It is not good for anything any longer but to be thrown out and trodden underfoot by men.

[14]You are the light of the world. A city set on a hill cannot be hidden

We give flavor to those who are seeking Him and provide the seasoning required to exercise our faith muscles. This flavoring allows us to be the disciplined ones He has called us to be in order that we may operate in the righteous things of God. Operating in the ways of righteousness enables us to delve into the deeper things that He wishes for us to see. Each of our steps is ordained but if we are not walking in His pre ordained steps, then we are walking in the opposite direction and turning back, despite the fact that we are told not to do such things.

2 Peter 2:21-22

[21]It would have been better for them not to have known the way of righteousness, than to have known it and then to turn their backs on the sacred command that was passed on to them. [22]Of them the proverbs are true: "A dog returns to its vomit,"[f] and, "A sow that is washed goes back to her wallowing in the mud."

Looking back and moving forward are opposites and therefore, we cannot walk in righteousness, if we are always looking back. God has called us away from that life. Just as in Sodom and Gomorrah God is showing us, that where we used to be is not for us anymore. If whatever it is in at the back of us, then we are to realize our positioning and accept where He has us in this moment of time. We are to be concentrating on where He is taking us. The events that happened yesterday, or last month or last year, is indicative that God does not want us there any longer. He has moved on and therefore so should we. We are to be moving forward with the things that He has set aside for us for our own protection and safety.

Just like the Israelites in the desert, we cannot use yesterday's manna for today's bread.

Each day the Lord provides us with Himself, so that we can see a new side of Him; a new side of His mercies and His grace.

We should not however use His grace as a means of not moving forward in the things of God or as an excuse to keep ourselves where we are in life. In fact it is the very opposite.

Grace is the oil that keeps our spiritual engine running, when it is mixed with the fuel of the Holy Spirit.

Often we hear the term that we are saved by grace. If this was taken in the proper context, then all of us could just continue to be disobedient to the commands of God and we would never take hold of the destiny He has before us.

We use grace as a reason to stay the way we are and an excuse not to operate in His purpose. Instead of rising up to God's level, we demote ourselves by having more belief in what we can see rather than in what we deny to observe.

The fact that Lot's wife ended, shows us that grace was not given when she knowingly was in direct disobedience to the command of God. In this case there was no time to repent and start over. Having said that how many commands have you been given that you put off and used the excuse " Well I'm just a sinner saved by grace," so that you did not have to face what you had done in disobedience?

What does saved by grace mean?
Saved By Grace

- In simple terms grace first of all is another word for favor.
- It is the saving grace of God that enables you to go to Him in the first place.
- It's His grace that enables you to pray or you wouldn't be able to pray.
- It's His grace that enables you to keep pursuing and overtaking

- It's His grace that motivates your spirit.

- It's His grace that allows you to seek Him every day.
- Without Him you cannot do anything.
- Without Him you do not have any grace to get anything done.
- It's His grace that pushes you forward into the things of God.
- You are saved from the distractions that keep you from fulfilling His purpose.
- Only by His grace can you continue to do the assignment that God has called you to do.
- You are a sinner saved by grace because when Jesus died on the cross He has you covered.

What does have you covered mean? It means that when you accept the fact that Jesus died on the cross for you sins, He is telling you "I know you are trying, but just in case you don't get it right, I got you covered."

This is the operation of grace.

When we continually manifest His Kingdom on earth, it is His grace that covers us as a shield so that we can continue to endure our process that leads into our assignment.

We don't have to worry about sin and dying in other words, because we are exercising our faith. Exercising our faith with correctness of heart and mind, is a testament to what we believe and serves a marker as to where we are going.

. Without the grace of Jesus dying on the cross you are not able to be the glove that He needs in order that others may see the manifestation of Christ in you.

. Without grace we would not be able to lose our life for Christ.

Without grace we would not be able to gain a new life for Him.

Luke 17: 32-33

³² Remember Lot's wife.
³³ Whosoever shall seek to gain his life shall lose it: but whosoever shall lose his life shall preserve it.

We are to seek the life that HE has for us, instead of searching the life that WE want for us. Therefore if we lose what we want for our lives and replace it with what God wants for our lives, we don't look back at what we THINK we should have, we look forward to what we KNOW we can have. It is better to be molded into His Image than to be molded into a pillar that exhibits no heavenly characteristics.

So therefore since we are all sinners, we are not eliminated from our divine assignments, rather we are empowered to do them.

Grace is the covering that allows us to fulfill His purpose in the earth. It is grace that allows us to give up our selfish selves and replace that with the things that are of Him so that others may have the same joy and benefit.

Acts 20:24-25 (New Living Translation)

[24] But my life is worth nothing to me unless I use it for finishing the work assigned me by the Lord Jesus—the work of telling others the Good News about the wonderful grace of God.

By not looking back at what used to be, we look forward to all we can be.

By not looking back we stay focused on what God has for us, not what we want for us.

By not looking back we remember where we used to be, but also remember we strive to where we are supposed to be.

By not looking back we are obedient to the Kingdom of God and disobedient to the ways of the world and Babylon.

By not looking back we are led by His Spirit and directed in His ways.

By not looking back we make the decision to honor God and glorify His name.

By not looking back, we promote the Kingdom of God.
The Kingdom of God is God's agenda.

What is Mine?

The King's Answer
The Earth Is Mine and the Fullness Thereof

His Royal Agenda Part 8

Hear Ye, Hear Ye

**Everything I Have
Is The Lord's**

Everything I Have Is On Loan From Heaven!
Psalm 24:1-3 (The Message)

1-2 God claims Earth and everything in it, God claims World and all who live on it. He built it on Ocean foundations, laid it out on River girders. 3-4 Who can climb Mount God? Who can scale the holy north-face? Only the clean-handed, only the pure-hearted; Men who won't cheat, women who won't seduce.

Everything we have the Lord has given us. From the very breath we take to the roofs we have over our head, we must acknowledge that the Lord owns it all. We would not be here if we were not sent here in the first place. We would not do what we do, if we were not given the opportunity to do so.

Within all the things that God has given us, the most important is faith. Faith is not a noun but a verb. We confuse the words religious affiliation with faith.

Faith is God given and everyone has a measure of it.

Faith combined with submission is necessary for our spirit to grow to levels we have not known. Acknowledging who God is, allows us to be reflected back to His image. When we truly see His image, we see who we are when we look at Him.

Looking at Him is necessary in order to acknowledge who He is in the correct manner. The way we look at Him and ourselves is evident in our thought life. How we act is directly connected to the thoughts that we have of Him and our actions closely follow.

Our acknowledgement that the earth is the Lord's, brings us into agreement with Him, as we look each day with newness in Spirit and in Truth. When looked at correctly, we see the awesome majesty of how good He is, even when times are rough.

When we look at Him as sovereign, we understand that everything that we go through is closely watched by the Lord. He sends out His word and makes sure that the angels are dispatched to be sure that His Word is fulfilled.

Each Word is sent to provide the circumstances and the provision necessary for us to complete the assignment that is on each of our lives. Submission to His authority needs to be constant and in essence should be made a priority on a daily and minute basis.

A true disciple must be disciplined and submission and acknowledgement that everything is the Lord's, provides a foundation for us to work upwards from.

Being commanded to be servants is necessary in holding Him as sovereign. He is the One who gave us authority on this earth, but the earth is still the Lord's. God is King and everyone and everything is subject to Him. He knows how every plant, animal and being exists in this earth since He is the One who created all.

Lucifer does not want to acknowledge the Lord God, but he still has to submit to what the Lord says. He cannot go beyond the boundaries that have been set forth. He is not allowed to tempt you beyond what you can bear and he cannot kill you.

We are not to acknowledge his involvement in our lives but rather look at how God is using him to squeeze gifting out of ours. We are to look at the strengths we are building and the Godly characteristics that need to be developed so that we can more look like Him.

Our thoughts must come under constant submission and obedience. If we cannot bring our thoughts under the Lord's submission, how can we say we are being obedient to God. When our thoughts are out of order and we at the same time try to demonstrate God's kingdom ways, we establish a hypocritical pride that God hates. God wishes for us to give of all of ourselves to His submission, so that we are not seen as hypocrites but as true disciples. Many can talk but few can walk properly. Instead of walking with great strength and confidence, we hide the demonic prosthetics that make us look holy rather than being holy. In this sense we do not have or exhibit any divine power that is needed to transform lives for His Kingdom.

2 Timothy 3

¹But mark this: There will be terrible times in the last days. ²People will be lovers of themselves, lovers of money, boastful, proud, abusive, disobedient to their parents, ungrateful, unholy, ³without love, unforgiving, slanderous, without self-control, brutal, not lovers of the good, ⁴treacherous, rash, conceited, lovers of pleasure rather than lovers of God— ⁵having a form of godliness but denying its power. Have nothing to do with them.

Jesus died and presented Himself as a living sacrifice. We are to do the same. We are to die to ourselves and present ourselves as a living sacrifice as well, so that we are able to do what He has commissioned us to do. We cannot accept His sacrifice unless we die to ourselves first. If we do not, then we give lip service and end up living defeated lives which are void of any good fruit and lives that do not affect the kingdom. We end up building kingdoms in our minds of where we ourselves rule in ungodly authority.

We end up worshipping ourselves by wanting what we want instead of what God wants for us. Through this behavior we disallow the honor that should be God's and place it on ourselves. We should remember however that if we want to be our own god, then we must take responsibility of what it takes to be one.

When we become our own god, we take on the traits of Lucifer himself by exhibiting and mirroring his image upon the earth. We honor ourselves and place God on the back burner. Then we call Him up when we figure we need His help. Thus we don't honor Him with the proper honor which is due. We insult Him but wanting Him to bow down to our level so that we can attain a kingdom of greed and lust.

When we do not acknowledge God as sovereign Lord, we start to believe that we are better than everyone else and that our ways are much better than God's. We think just because we forget about God's presence in the physical, that He does the same and is not cognizant of what we ar doing and how we are behaving.

We look at ourselves as pious and in this severe state of rebellion we dare get angry with Him. All this because we cannot have the evil thing that He has protected us from in the first place. Our desires thus are not aligned with His and therefore the acknowledgements belonging to Him are null and void.

It is then that we try to camouflage how we really feel, by making excuses for our shortcomings, rather than facing the reasons of why we have not moved forward. Lying to ourselves delays our movement forward into the things that await us in destiny.

We live arrogant, sinful and prideful lives because we do not want to give God the honor that is He alone is due. When we are out of order then everything in our lives will be out of order.

When we realize that honor is given from the top to the bottom, we stop living "giving honor from the bottom to the top."

When we give honor from the bottom to the top, we end up worshipping the creation rather than the creator.

Idle or Idol worship is the thing that places itself before God. Whatever we worship becomes the focal point in our lives and every thought is molded around it.

Whatever we worship we make a constant thought in our minds that is driven by our pride and ego. Whatever we worship then takes over our lives and causes us to live in a dimension that is so dangerous that God alone should be the only One there.

When we worship ourselves we have no repentance and no remorse for any wrongdoings. When we worship ourselves we hold the deadly sins that Jesus died to take away. We must remember that Jesus died for our sins and if it is a gift should, we take it. When we worship ourselves and what He has created rather than the Creator, we give back the gift of His death and thus we crucify ourselves by our own thoughts and actions. Someone has to die for sin. It can be you or you can choose to take Jesus death as a gift so that you don't have to.

When we choose to live in sin, then we become our own god and as a god should be accepting of all that the job has to offer. Being a god requires you take the responsibilities of both good and bad.

That being said, we are made fully aware of who God is and who we are in His sight. The basic believing in Him should be the foundational standard that we use to train our minds in His kingdom. Believing is not the mere saying that yes I know He exists for even Satan himself believes. It is the doing that backs up our belief system that is paramount in what Jesus said when we are to believe.

When we believe in God correctly, we see ourselves correctly. Often there are many misplaced people in congregations today, because of what they have been taught to believe. When they are misplaced, they become angry because they think they deserve better, when all along they could be very well in the right place but with the wrong perception. Thus when the correct perception is not there, then everything else will be out of balance.

We are all different parts of Christ's body. One of the tools Satan uses in God's people is to throw their perception off. The first way to throw their perception off is to get them to get their minds off of the fullness of God and onto the fullness of themselves.

It is no wonder that they then give Satan so much credit for what he does in their lives, because they actually come into agreement with what he has to offer them. Satan has the ability to make you feel correct about a person or situation, because of the lustful ways that drive him.

In obedience to him, you then adopt those same ways and when you find out he lied to you; you end up blaming God for something He did not want you to be part of in the first place.

When we are out of alignment, we end up resenting God when He enforces discipline. Being out of alignment then causes our thoughts to be in disorder, and therefore we place ourselves into a position we are not to be placed, rather than have God place us.

We are all part of one body and we cannot be a leg if God has ordained us to be an arm. We cannot be a mouth if God ordained us to be a foot.

Romans 12

A Living Sacrifice to God
¹ And so, dear brothers and sisters, I plead with you to give your bodies to God because of all he has done for you. Let them be a living and holy sacrifice—the kind he will find acceptable. This is truly the way to worship him. ² Don't copy the behavior and customs of this world, but let God transform you into a new person by changing the way you think. Then you will learn to know God's will for you, which is good and pleasing and perfect.

³ Because of the privilege and authority God has given me, I give each of you this warning: Don't think you are better than you really are. Be honest in your evaluation of yourselves, measuring yourselves by the faith God has given us. ⁴ Just as our bodies have many parts and each part has a special function, ⁵ so it is with Christ's body. We are many parts of one body, and we all belong to each other.

It is so important to acknowledge and believe God is our creator and is in charge of everything. It is easier then to submit to His authority, rather than have to come up against it.

When we realize that He lives in every one of us, we are able to see the God in them rather than just the creation itself. God is love and it is that love that He wants us to exhibit to others.

God's love is:

1 Corinthians 13:3-5 (New International Version)

³If I give all I possess to the poor and surrender my body to the flames, but have not love, I gain nothing.
⁴Love is patient, love is kind. It does not envy, it does not boast, it is not proud. ⁵It is not rude, it is not self-seeking, it is not easily angered, it keeps no record of wrongs.

When we are in agreement with Satan rather than being in alignment with God, we give Satan the permission to penetrate our thoughts and permission to direct our lives. We give him the honor that is due God and gain a warped sense of what love is all about.

God is love and since He Himself is a living demonstration of that love, we know how we are to imitate that same love. Once again, the first is the acknowledgement of His sovereignty and the second is the action of our faith that starts from within our hearts.

What is Faith?

Hebrews 11

¹Now faith is the substance of things hoped for, the evidence of things not seen.

It is also:

F-Fire **A**-Applied **I**-In **T**-The **H**-Heart

We cannot exercise faith if we do not operate in God's love. You cannot exercise faith without it, because love is the spiritual hydraulics that carry the burdens that come with faith.

If God is persistent in our thoughts we follow through in our actions. They will replicate Him. If we honor Satan we have the opposite. What should be love then becomes an obsession. The definition of obsession is:

    a persistent disturbing preoccupation with an often unreasonable idea or feeling; *broadly*: compelling motivation

Any thought or action that does not line up with God's sovereignty has the ability to turn into an obsession. In other words we become preoccupied with the things of ourselves that are based in Satan's rule.

Since the definition is a disturbing preoccupation with an unreasonable idea or feeling, we should think of the following.

If the earth is the Lord's and everything in it is God's, then isn't it unreasonable to think that we can come against that kind of power and authority? In other words, if what we are thinking is not of God, it takes authority in our lives instead of us allowing God to take authority. We not only end up with a preoccupation with selfish and demonic thoughts, but we pay homage to its effects. How? By getting joy out of selfishness, instead of the joy of righteousness.

God then sees our faith by what we put trust in. We put ourselves on dangerous ground however, when God chooses to show you the strength of your foundation.

God will test our faith, whether it is based in Him or based on ourselves. Either way it will be tested. It is with the testing that He sees His trust level in us. In the same manner, we see for ourselves how much we can be entrusted with as well.

God wants to be able to trust us with dominion just as He did with Adam. He demonstrates through testing how much He trusts us. He tests our obedience and where our true love really lies.

God Sees behind Appearances

Luke 16: 10-18

[10-13]Jesus went on to make these comments: If you're honest in small things, you'll be honest in big things; If you're a crook in small things,

you'll be a crook in big things. If you're not honest in small jobs, who will put you in charge of the store? No worker can serve two bosses: He'll either hate the first and love the second Or adore the first and despise the second. You can't serve both God and the Bank.

¹⁴⁻¹⁸When the Pharisees, a money-obsessed bunch, heard him say these things, they rolled their eyes, dismissing him as hopelessly out of touch. So Jesus spoke to them: "You are masters at making yourselves look good in front of others, but God knows what's behind the appearance. What society sees and calls monumental, God sees through and calls monstrous. God's Law and the Prophets climaxed in John; Now it's all kingdom of God—the glad news and compelling invitation to every man and woman. The sky will disintegrate and the earth dissolve before a single letter of God's Law wears out.

God wants us to be ever persistent in maintaining His presence in our lives. We are His possession and with that comes certain responsibilities. Many people want the prophets to prophecy to them, but few of them want to do what is necessary in order to attain what God has spoken through the prophet. God does not change. He is sovereign and all things including each and every one of us belong to Him. When we acknowledge Him we come into the agreement that we are His possession.

Exodus 19:5

⁵'*Now then, if you will indeed obey My voice and keep My covenant, then you shall be My own possession among all the peoples, for all the earth is Mine;*

Deuteronomy 10:14

¹⁴"*Behold to the LORD your God belong heaven and the highest heavens, the earth and all that is in it.*

1 Corinthians 10:26

²⁶FOR THE EARTH IS THE LORD'S, AND ALL IT CONTAINS.

Our power lies in His power. Our submission dictates how much power the Lord can entrust us with. God will place His ordered ones in front of us to see if we are able to act in accordance, to the true God in Him. In order to do this however we must know who He is to begin with. We must know His characteristics and learn His ways, so that we are able to recognize Him, when He shows up.

Many will say they submit to Him but they will not submit to their fellow man. They speak Godly, while their actions are selfish and demonic. They find excuses to stay the same instead of operating in the kingdom manner we are called to do. Their focus is on themselves and their money. They build storehouses for the kingdoms of this world instead of the Kingdom of God.

Luke 16

¹⁴⁻¹⁸When the Pharisees, a money-obsessed bunch, heard him say these things, they rolled their eyes, dismissing him as hopelessly out of touch. So Jesus spoke to them: "You are masters at making yourselves look good in front of others, but God knows what's behind the appearance.

They do not delight in the Lord and because of that lack their lives reflect the kingdom of darkness rather than the Kingdom of Light. Anyone that does not come into agreement with what the Lord would deem as hypocrites are devalued in their eyes and are made to feel as if they don't know what they are doing.

These same people may even rebel to the point of saying "they can't tell me what to do." They think they know better and treat others in a negative way, when the golden rule says to love others as you.

If you love others as yourself as Jesus said, then others will know how much you love others by how you perceive yourself. If you are not doing things right, then I should know that you won't treat me right, because you are not treating yourself correctly.

If we look at one another and see how we treat others, then we see whom that person acknowledges as supreme in their lives. Anyone operating in the kingdom thus knows who his ruler or King is, because his life reflects the assignment that the king has placed on his or her life. Therefore you can accept God's assignment, Satan's assignment or your own.

When we acknowledge that all things are under God, then everyone and everything we become involved with is under God. When we believe this statement we flow in His divinity instead of demonic activity.

We exercise the God out of us by the faith that He has placed in us. Faith is the only thing we own. (Salvation is a gift once we receive it.) How much faith we own is up to us.

We know how much we own by how much we use on day to day basis. We know how close we are to God, when our faith is tested. We know how strong how faith muscles are by how much they are exercised. Since faith is in us and love is in our hearts, how appropriate that faith is a muscle just as the heart is. God wants you to acknowledge Him in the now, because He is a now God.

All the earth is the Lord's. He owns everything, but He did give us faith to take ownership of. It is that measure of faith that He has placed to be according to the assignment He has given to us to fulfill. It is that measure of faith that He expects for us to go to Him every day, so He can exercise Himself in us.

We are His and His alone. It is up to us to submit to Him and His kingdom so we can establish His order. We are to love Him and reject sin. We are to be possessed by Him and not obsessed by Satan or ourselves. We are to be so in love with Him that the very idea of sin is disgusting to us. We need to be in the place where God is sovereign and we are to take great joy in all the things He has given us to have dominion over.

Everything comes from Him and all through Him all things are given. What He gives we use for a time, so that we are able to do His work. When that time is over, we accept and move on because sometimes it's not beneficial for us to hang on to old things.

Therefore, everything we have is on loan. The only thing we own is our faith which is our belief system. All things in this life are temporary and in God all things are eternal. All things He gives to us therefore are the tools necessary to operate in the fullness of God upon this earth. Therefore it is in our best interest to acknowledge and believe that the earth is the Lord's and fullness thereof.

How Can I Get More Out of This Life?

The King's Answer
Promotion Comes From God

Royal Agenda Part Nine
Hear Ye, Hear Ye

I WILL PROMOTE OTHERS SO THAT GOD CAN PROMOTE ME

Scripture Reading "God makes war against the arrogant, but gives grace to the humble. Therefore, humble yourselves under the powerful hand of God that He may promote you at the proper time." ***1 Peter 5:5-6*** *"For not he who promotes himself is approved, but whom the Lord promotes."* ***2 Corinthians 10:18*** *"For everyone who exalts himself shall be humbled. And he who humbles himself shall be promoted."*** Luke 14:11*** *"Humble yourselves before the Lord and He will promote you."* ***James 4:10***

In the great infinite circle of life, the Lord gave His Son as an example of how to give outwardly. He starts with a setup of giving to those closest to you. In doing so we practice giving and thus promoting whom the Lord is within us.

Throughout biblical history, all those whom the Lord was paramount in their lives and those who chose to do God's will, always had the orders of the Lord to fulfill. In fulfilling these Kingdom orders, they had to put the people first instead of themselves. In a Kingdom the King always puts the people's needs first. He is the One who must keep His covenant with His people and is also the One whom they must rely.

Giving others what they need promotes who they are while at the same time promotes the Kingdom of God within you. Giving however does not in any way mean that you are to leave yourself with nothing, because you are to treat others as yourself. In this way, we imitate and mirror the image of God. Just as He gave us Jesus, we are to give of ourselves. The Father gave His only Son, His own, His body. We are to do the same for Him and become that mirrored image He so desires of us.

Luke 6:31

Whatever you want people to do for you, do the same for them.

Luke 6:31 (The Message)

³¹⁻³⁴"Here is a simple rule of thumb for behavior: Ask yourself what you want people to do for you; then grab the initiative and do it for them! If you only love the lovable, do you expect a pat on the back? Run-of-the-mill sinners do that. If you only help those who help you, do you expect a medal? Garden-variety sinners do that. If you only give for what you hope to get out of it, do you think that's charity? The stingiest of pawnbrokers does that.

Human kind needs an example and a manifestation of who Christ is upon this earth. Not being that example only promotes blasphemy against the cross and promotes the idea that His death was irrelevant. The cross holds power and if we do not acknowledge that power exists then how can we operate in it's benefits.

We must remember that the Kingdom of God lives within us. That internal life must bring life to others in order that Christ may be manifested to those who do not know Him. In promoting others so that we can be promoted, we become a living miracle that others will be able to witness and we manifest a grace and power that can only come from God.

The Lord not only wants us to promote people we know, but especially our enemies and the people we don't know.

When we promote the people we know, this may be a good deed, but more importantly when we promote our enemies, we offer our bodies as a sacrifice just as Jesus did. At Jesus crucifixion as He was being put to death by His enemies, He at the same time was promoting them through it. Without the death He had to experience, they would not be able to promote others, for His grace would not have been available without the price which had to be paid. He looked at others and in accordance we must do the same.

Philippians 2:4

Look not every man on his own things, but every man also on the things of others

Promoting others first is promoting His Kingdom first; for what we do for others and the Kingdom, God will do for us. By promoting others we diminish the selfishness in our lives. In doing what is required we will have the order and structure we need to exercise the will of the Lord. When the world dictates that "it's every man for himself" we should be an example of "its everyone for Himself."

If we actually obeyed the latter we would not only expand the Kingdom, but we would begin to roll a ball that would steadily grow in momentum.

When we promote others we are givers not only of our time, but of our thoughts and actions. We do not become a burden when we give, we become a blessing. In essence we should ask ourselves if we wish to be a burden or blessing.

We should not seek what belongs to others for in doing so we look and act like the world. The world seeks after its own interests which are temporal. Kingdom people seek after what is eternal.

Philippians 2:21
[21]For they all seek after their own interests, not those of Christ Jesus.

Seeking after the temporal things of this world not only steals from the Kingdom, but also places disorder in our thinking and in our actions. When we do not promote others we set ourselves up to be a burden upon others and ourselves. The world operates on a level that humans need to feed their selfish wants and desires. They end up chasing wrong things at the wrong time or chasing the right things at the wrong time.

Within families these actions not only steal from a child's inheritance, but also rob future generations of correct thinking and subsequent blessings. This disorder places the burden on the children to give to the parents instead of the parents giving to the children.

The parents thus become a burden to their children when they are supposed to be a launch pad for their promotion.

This behavior enables lessons learned by the children that end up being taught to future generations. They live in the present set of circumstances instead of having the mind of Christ; who by His own example shows the extent of how we are to promote our families.

They end up making a short term decision to a long term problem. When these decisions are made then all else fails.

2 Corinthians 12:14

14Here for this third time Iam ready to come to you, and I will not be a burden to you; for I (do not seek what is yours, but you; for children are not responsible to save up for their parents, but parents for their children.

The principle is simple. Promoting those close to you such as your children, enables you to promote others without motive. If you do not promote your own children with saved blessings, you cannot promote others with the same mindset. You will end up promoting others with wrong motives, because your motives have already been established at home. It is easy for you to take this simple test.

When was the last time you promoted someone that you did not get any gratification personally? When you helped someone, what selfish joy did you get out of it? What motives backed your reason to help or promote someone else? Did you do something that looked spiritual but had worldly backing? Did you do a good deed because it allowed you to get some personal joy or gain out of it? Did you want to look good? Did you just want to go along for the ride because you had nothing else to do? Did you promote because someone gave you some glory because of it? How much did you talk about helping someone after the fact?

Perhaps we should look and see when we did something on purpose for God, while simultaneously promoting someone and getting absolutely nothing in return. We should try and promote without expecting a single word of thanks or payment. We are to do simply because it is expected of us. This behavior eliminates the want of worldly power and demonic influence. It stops our egos from getting engorged with pride and helps in the destruction of our fleshly desires. It places the right spirit necessary to be able to serve our fellow man.

Matthew 20:26

24-28When the ten others heard about this, they lost their tempers, thoroughly disgusted with the two brothers. So Jesus got them together to settle things down. He said, "You've observed how godless rulers throw their weight around, how quickly a little power goes to their heads. It's not going to be that way with you. Whoever wants to be great must become a servant. Whoever wants to be first among you must be your slave. That is what the Son of Man has done: He came to serve, not be served—and then to give away his life in exchange for the many who are held hostage."

We should try and promote others when it takes some pain to do so. Just as Jesus experienced pain in His promotion, we truly do not promote until we experience some sort of sacrificial pain, so that the Father may give us the grace needed to do so. When we promote, it moves God to give us grace. When you promote others and become their servant, you set yourself up to receive grace from God.

James 4:6

⁶But He gives a greater grace Therefore it says, "GOD IS OPPOSED TO THE PROUD, BUT GIVES GRACE TO THE HUMBLE."

The worldly system dictates that we should put what we want and need first, but in the Kingdom, God wishes to place others before us. The Lord deals with the wealth of His people on a totally different level than how the world does it.

The globe is in chaos because of the worldly system and the operators of it. The world says be greedy and keep everything for you. Do things our way and you will be rewarded with even more greed and corruption.Promote our agenda and we will keep your stuff safe for awhile.

God's Kingdom declares for us to give and cause others to do well ahead of you. When we do this we are able to see the substantial blessing that is coming to us. In other words, when we promote someone else, we are able to see the blessing that has been given out of us, In reciprocation we are also able to see His Will when it abounds back to us.

We can only have what we can see with our spiritual eye. The next time you promote someone, look at the level of God in you. For it is the Lord in you that allows you to promote others and it's the Lord in someone else that gives it back to you. It is the Lord that works the divine circumstances that enables you to be in the right place at the right time for the right blessing in the right moment.

Therefore we should not be seeking our own wealth, but rather should be helping someone else get theirs, so that we are able to receive ours.

1 Corinthians 10:24

Let no man seek his own, but every man another's wealth.

If we really love our fellow man in the way the Lord expects us to, we will promote him to the best that our faith allows us. If we only want for ourselves, then we stop God from advancing us. When we only advance ourselves, we have no need of God for we are operating in our own worldly power and not the Lords.

Promotion in His Kingdom is not being a mere blessing to others, but includes the teaching of others for edification of kingdom citizens.

We are all chosen to be Kingdom citizens. It is up to us to operate in this kingdom in the manner He purposes. Any other method of operation is not of God and promotes the worldly system. Our lives should reflect what we have learned and we promote others by actually doing what the Lord has commanded. Since all of us are not literal teachers, our lives and our conduct should reflect our God and through it others may learn and be spiritually guided and promoted.

We then begin to learn that the more we do these things, the more they have become part of our personality and makeup. Since others learn and observe this we set them up in order to propel them forward into the things of God.

Their spiritual well being then affects every aspect of their lives, as the Lord moves in their everyday circumstances. It is then that we are positioned in place to be a support on their destined journey.

This brings glory to the One who deserves it in the first place. It is His power that enables you to be a living epistle and it's His power that does more than we can ask or imagine.

Ephesians 3:20 (Contemporary English Version)

20-21I pray that Christ Jesus and the church will forever bring praise to God. His power at work in us can do far more than we dare ask or imagine. Amen.

Therefore promoting others is not a game or race to see who can do a better job at excelling others or how many brownie points we can score.

God is looking at our motives and our hidden agendas to see how much of Himself working is working in you.

We are His children and He wishes us to keep those same childlike characteristics when we are older. The world institutes a set of standards that make children grow up too fast. When a child grows up too fast, they lose their innocence and their circumstances often cause them to be disassociated with trust.

I believe that this is why in this generation, that children are exposed to things that parents or elders should only have the capability of experiencing.

In the Kingdom, children remain innocent and they trust their spiritual Father to bless and keep them. There is no in fighting or positioning in order to receive from Him. They do what is requested of them because it was asked of them. There is no corruption in their thinking and no hidden motives in their responsive answers.

Matthew 18:1-5 (New American Standard Bible)
Rank in the Kingdom

¹At that time the disciples came to Jesus and said, "Who then is greatest in the kingdom of heaven?"
²And He called a child to Himself and set him before them,
³and said, "Truly I say to you, unless you are converted and become like children, you will not enter the kingdom of heaven.
⁴"Whoever then humbles himself as this child, he is the greatest in the kingdom of heaven.

Thus, the Lord asks that we promote others instead of ourselves. In doing this we promote the things of God and the desires of ourselves.

Luke 22:26

²⁶"But it is not this way with you, but the one who is the greatest among you must become like the youngest, and the leader like the servant.

Matthew 23:12

12 (A) Whoever exalts himself shall be humbled; and whoever humbles himself shall be exalted.

The Definition of humble is as follows: It comes from the Hebrew word Shachach, which means to bow, crouch, bow down, be bowed down.

- To be bowed down, be prostrated, be humbled
- To bow (in homage)
- To bow (of mourner)
- To crouch (of wild beast in lair)
- To be prostrated, be humbled, be reduced, be weakened, proceed humbly, be bowed down
- To prostrate, lay low, bow down
- To be cast down, be despairing

In other words He who bows down to the Lords commands is one who is in obedience to Him, regardless of what we personally think or say. We control our speech in order that it may not deter someone and we act in accordance with what is beneficial for others to grow.

Our actions become synonymous with His and we become the manifestation of the prayer that was prayed. Like a pinball machine we become the bumpers necessary to accelerate the ball to the upward position in order to enter the destined point.

Promoting others is the giving away of what we want so that we can see the manifestation of God in others. Promoting others allows us to physically see the Kingdom of God working in us. Promoting others is necessary for our own promotion. We are not to tire of doing it over and over again.

Galatians 6:9 (The Message)

9-10So let's not allow ourselves to get fatigued doing good. At the right time we will harvest a good crop if we don't give up, or quit. Right now, therefore, every time we get the chance, let us work for the benefit of all, starting with the people closest to us in the community of faith.

Promotion comes from God alone. When it is your turn to be promoted God will see to it that it gets done. When it's time for a promotion He often times uses an enemy to promote you so that justice is served. All of us need to be promoted by someone else. Even Jesus was promoted by John the Baptist.

John the Baptist cried out in the desert for others to follow Jesus long before Jesus ministry went public. He knew that he must decrease for Jesus to increase. John knew that he had to humble himself so that God could exalt him. John had to decrease so that all attention could be on Christ. He had to decrease because there was only one Head needed and that was the Godhead that appeared at Jesus baptism.

John was beheaded for natural and symbolic reasons. He was beheaded because Herod's daughter wanted his head on a platter, but also for the spiritual reasons. You cannot have two heads in a ministry that are going in the opposite direction. John had to sit down and Jesus had to rise up. In this sense anything with more than two heads is a beast. That is not the image that the Lord wants us looking toward.

Therefore John was humbled and the Lord called him the greatest prophet that ever lived. He not only announced Jesus but made a way for others to follow Him so that they could receive the Kingdom of God.

He knew why and for what purpose He was born. After He completed the destiny God had chosen for Him, Jesus showed Himself personally, so that John would have no doubt in his mind that he had done what was required. He knew he was designed for that specific moment in time.

John 3:30 (The Message)

29-30"That's why my cup is running over. This is the assigned moment for him to move into the center, while I slip off to the sidelines.

Something to think about is this: God wants to promote His people.

How many will you promote with no hidden motives? Would you be able to put your life on the line if the Lord required for the benefit of someone else's life?

How much are you willing to give up so that others can give you what you require?

How much do you trust God in the process of giving others their promotion?

Each time someone in the bible has promoted others, God has given His glory to shine upon that individual.

Jesus promoted us by dying on the cross. He put us first before Himself.

Judas promoted Jesus by promoting himself. By promoting himself he experienced destruction. He was not only one of Jesus' followers, but also one of His enemies. God still used Judas to propel His Son into destiny. In that manner, Judas lived up to the destiny he was to fulfill.

John the Baptist promoted Jesus and He seen God and His promises.

Abraham promoted Lot and God gave Abraham the generations of the earth.

Joseph's brothers promoted him by leaving him to die in a pit. God retrieved Joseph and in the end, Joseph's brothers were in the palace.

Promoting others the Kingdom way allows God's glory to be seen as it should. If we are obedient to the task in the way He has determined, we not only fulfill the obedience we are called unto, but we are a testament to others to prove to them that God's word works.

When we give ourselves glory we pump up our egos and the rewards are but in a moment. When we glorify God it shows others we know Him and that He is real and operating in our everyday lives.

John 8:53-55 (New International Version)

[53]Are you greater than our father Abraham? He died, and so did the prophets. Who do you think you are?"
[54]Jesus replied, "If I glorify myself, my glory means nothing. My Father, whom you claim as your God, is the one who glorifies me. [55]Though you do not know him, I know him. IfI said I did not, I would be a liar like you, but I do know him and keep his word.

We need to stand out and be the manifestation of God working in and through us. We need to be ourselves and not put on a show in order to receive acceptance or get what we think for our own promotion; We need to be the people God has called us to be. This would be our true self. It's not the person the world has dictated as to who you are, but of whom God said you are.

This kingdom mindset promotes your thinking so that you are able to function the way God intended. He brings you to the forefront at the appropriate and destined time.

What man gives you, man can take away, but what God gives you, you are not only able to keep. You will have so much you will be a blessing to others and God will get all the glory. Stay in order and maintain the ability to promote others.

Matthew 23:11

11-12"Do you want to stand out? Then step down. Be a servant. If you puff yourself up, you'll get the wind knocked out of you. But if you're content to simply be yourself, your life will count for plenty.

Jesus' Prayer For You

John 17:1-12 (The Message)

1-5 Jesus said these things. Then, raising his eyes in prayer, he said: Father, it's time. Display the bright splendor of your Son So the Son in turn may show your bright splendor. You put him in charge of everything human So he might give real and eternal life to all in his charge. And this is the real and eternal life: That they know you, The one and only true God, And Jesus Christ, whom you sent. I glorified you on earth By completing down to the last detail What you assigned me to do. And now, Father, glorify me with your very own splendor, The very splendor I had in your presence Before there was a world. 6-121 spelled out your character in detail To the men and women you gave me. They were yours in the first place; Then you gave them to me, And they have now done what you said. They know now, beyond the shadow of a doubt, That everything you gave me is firsthand from you, For the message you gave me, I gave them; And they took it, and were convinced That I came from you. They believed that you sent me. I pray for them. I'm not praying for the God-rejecting world But for those you gave me, For they are yours by right. Everything mine is yours, and yours mine, And my life is on display in them. For I'm no longer going to be visible in the world; They'll continue in the world While I return to you. Holy Father, guard them as they pursue this life That you conferred as a gift through me, So they can be one heart and mind As we are one heart and mind. As long as I was with them, I guarded them In the pursuit of the life you gave through me; I even posted a night watch. And not one of them got away, Except for the rebel bent on destruction (the exception that proved the rule of Scripture).

What Do I Need To Do?

The King's Answer
My Will Needs To Be Done

Royal Agenda Part Ten
Hear Ye, Hear Ye

**Thy Will Be Done
On Earth as it is in Heaven**

God downloads much like a computer. Data is sent at high rates through the airwaves, through the atmosphere. It's digital and wireless communication. Like a cell phone He speaks with no connected lines. We have to clear the interference and the static from religion and vain imaginations. We need to clear the distractions and do what God has called us to do.

It's time to be in sync.

It's just you and God.

When Jesus was baptized, He fulfilled the command through the presence of the Holy Spirit. He then worked and was able to perform the recorded miracles.

It did not take Him long to do what God wanted Him to do. Once in order and filled with God's Holy Spirit He was sent to show us how it's done in heaven. Now we must do as He did! We have to drop our old selves and move into synchronization with Him.

Synchronize is defined as anything that is happening at the same time; to represent or arrange (events) to indicate coincidence or coexistence; to make synchronous in operation; happening, existing, or arising at precisely the same time : recurring or operating at exactly the same periods involving or indicating synchronism; having the same period; also: having the same period and phase: geostationary : of, used in, or being digital communication (as between computers) in which a common timing signal is established that dictates when individual bits can be transmitted and which allows for very high rates of data transfer.

God is a synchronizer. A synchronizer is like someone that makes sound line up with action like in the movies.

We are to be in sync with the commands of God. Anything that is not in sync is out of order. Therefore when He moves we move, when He talks, we talk, when He walks, we walk. When we do in this manner, the manifestation of God takes place and what we used to think were miracles become a supernatural way of life.

You must be in order for synchronization to take place. You have to be in time, in perfect time, in harmonious time. There is a new sound coming from the heavens. It is the sound of the Spirit rushing from Heaven. There is a Word coming from the wind, the atmosphere and He is saying come up here so I can show you what I see; so you can see what I see and when you see what I see, you can say what I say and when you say what I say, you will see what I see.

There is a new sound coming from heaven. There is a new sound coming from the heavens. It is the sound of the Spirit rushing from Heaven. There is a Word coming like the sound of many thunders saying come closer so you can hear what I hear. And when you hear what I hear, you can speak what you hear.

Experience, My breath for it is the sound of "H" in your "ear". This means that you will hear my Spirit in your ear. You will hear what my Spirit is saying and you will be able to do what you hear. No more waiting. You will hear and do in synchronization. You will see and hear what I speak and say, and simultaneously do it.

You will bring heaven upon the earth for the manifestation of the Glory of God. So do as I do, say as I say and you will produce what I see and what I say.

It is time (chronos). You were placed in time for such a time as this. All creation is waiting for you.

When Jesus did as His Father, what we see as miracles is just God's will in heaven. Many more will we also do.

John 14:12 (The Message)

[11-14]*"Believe me: I am in my Father and my Father is in me. If you can't believe that, believe what you see—these works. The person who trusts me will not only do what I'm doing but even greater things, because I, on my way to the Father, am giving you the same work to do that I've been doing. You can count on it. From now on, whatever you request along the lines of who I am and what I am doing, I'll do it. That's*

how the Father will be seen for who he is in the Son. I mean it. Whatever you request in this way, I'll do.

We don't co-exist with God. Meaning we are not separate. Jesus died for this reason so that we could. We exist with God. We are seated with Him in heaven. We operate in His authority which is in heaven. We rule beside Him in Spirit so that whatever is done in heaven is done on earth.

We do things on earth as they are done in heaven. We rule on the earth as God would rule in heaven. We each must learn how to possess the kingdom and rule in His authority. We must be in alignment in order to receive the scepter of ruling in righteousness. It is time to rule in the territory God has given you.

We don't have to be perfect through our own works; we just have to be in alignment and covenant with His Will. When our mindset is correct we are able to hear God's voice and empowered to advance His kingdom on this earth. His will is for us to operate in His will.

For this to take place, we must walk from the outer courtyard and into His throne room where kingdom matters are discussed.

It is once you are in alignment that you will hear and receive your spiritual orders. It is from His throne that you will be bestowed the royal crown of power that is only given to those of His Royal Family. From alignment to assignment on this earth, you will then be able to see what you loose on earth will be loosed in heaven, and what is loosed in heaven will be loosed on earth. You will be in sync with the Divine commands of God.

You will operate in the true dominion and power of His Royal Highness Our Lord and King. This power is given in order that you will rule with power, establish rule, and you will reign as your heavenly Father.

You are still here on earth. You are still alive. You may be down or you may have lost what you thought was everything. The mere fact you are still here, is validation that you are called for Divine purpose.

The Lord is not finished molding you yet to give you your special position of power and might.

Everything that you thought was evil, is just part of your training for kingship.

So lift up your head and look forward. What you thought was negative was just a setup from God. See with His eyes and look to where you are going. Your scepter is in His hand.

Since your scepter is in sight, you must now learn the ways of ruler ship and what is required to rule in the Kingdom of God. You must know what it is like to be a citizen in the Kingdom, as your life will dictated by the Father each and every moment of the day.

Now we must enter the throne room and receive the commands given by the Lord Himself in regards to how His governmental system operates. We must know the value of covenant and how to lay aside those things that cause us to be weak in the Kingdom of God.

We have learned some principles regarding kingdom living, but we must know how to enter into the kingdom in order to experience it fully. We have to learn what process is entailed and why not just anyone can enter on merit alone.

For here now we enter into the deeper things of God. We dig deep into how His kingdom operates and by the responsibilities He has given us. We must learn our rights in the Kingdom as well as our freedoms and liberties in Christ. We must learn what His Kingdom Constitution consists of in order to administer as proper ambassadors.

We must learn the things He requires since not just any man can enter into this place where we can rule with the correct order of His governmental authority.

We must learn about our King, His Prince and His Holy Spirit and rule from their perspective. All of this in order to obtain the keys of the kingdom and to rule with His approval.

Part II

Understanding Your Heavenly Heritage

Your Birthrights

Genesis 25:

²⁹⁻³⁰One day Jacob was cooking a stew. Esau came in from the
> field, starved. Esau said to Jacob, "Give me some of that red stew—I'm starved!" That's how he came to be called Edom (Red).
> ³ Jacob said, "Make me a trade: my stew for your rights as the firstborn."
> ³ Esau said, "I'm starving! What good is a birthright if I'm dead?"
> 33–34 Jacob said, "First, swear to me." And he did it. On oath Esau traded away his rights as the firstborn. Jacob gave him bread and the stew of lentils. He ate and drank, got up and left. That's how Esau shrugged off his rights as the firstborn.[1]

Looking at the story of how Esau traded away his birthright makes one wonder how he could have traded such a valuable inheritance for something so trivial. The story states that he traded red stew and that is how he became to be called Edom.

Edom means red. Red in biblical usage is the color of the earth from which Adam was made (Gen. 2:7; the letters for 'Adam' in Hebrew can also mean 'ruby,' and 'dust' can also mean 'reddish in color'), the color of Esau at birth (Gen. 25:25)

---

[1] Peterson, E. H. (2002). *The Message: The Bible in contemporary language* (Ge 25:29–34). Colorado Springs, Colo.: NavPress.

The rights of the firstborn were considered to be of more substantial value than the rest of the family would receive. There is a certain degree of high honor and prestige that go along with the material value of the inheritance which is granted to the firstborn. These rights and privileges are given to the receivers of such notable positions, for they have a right to more than their fair share in relation to other relatives and/or siblings.

The first-born' term, is used of people and animals; cognate terms being employed for firstfruits, and the first-born son's privileges and responsibilities are known as his 'birthright."

The first-born was regarded as 'the beginning of (his) strength' Gn. 49:3; Dt. 21:17; cf. Ps. 78:51; 105:36) and 'the opener of the womb' Ex. 13:2, 12, 15; Nu. 18:15; etc.), emphasizing both paternal and maternal lines. The pre-eminent status of first-born was also accorded to Israel (Ex. 4:22) and the Davidic line (Ps. 89:27).

The eldest son's special position was widely recognized in the ancient Near East. The accompanying privileges were highly valued, and in the OT included a larger inheritance, a special paternal blessing, family leadership and an honored place at mealtimes (Gn. 25:5–6; 27:35–36; 42:37; 43:33; Dt. 21:15–17).

Being firstborn was regarded as such a blessing and a privilege that no one in their proper mind would ever give up such a mark of favor.

When Esau (Of the earth) saw Jacob, he wanted instant gratification to sooth his flesh. His reasoning was that of "what good would it be to have a birthright or inheritance if you were not able to enjoy it."

In the prime desire of the moment he gave away what would have sustained him with a full and profitable life.

In a moment he traded with Jacob the blessing that had been passed down through generations. He gave it up or sold out for a pot of red stew.

The part we need to focus on is not that Jacob seized the moment, but that Esau gave away what suited his flesh. Esau was not aware of what was at stake. He didn't consider the ramifications of his actions.

He sold out what his Father wanted for him in exchange for what he wanted for himself. There is no difference in the gratification of the moment when compared to Adam and Eve in the Garden. They gave up a piece of fruit grown from the earth in exchange for their birthright.

He took for granted his birthright and his inheritance. Many today do the same thing. We are soon to give up our kingdom inheritance and authority for a second of gratification. We have become so wrapped up in this instant world that even the church has become a victim to its mindset.

When mistake the Word for the world. When we should be seeking, we just go to church and say, "feed me, feed me." When we get our bellies full, we get slothful and lazy and put our guards down. When opposition rises against us, we figure that no trouble should surround us. We live for lustful miracles moments and have become spiritually disabled, not able to walk in the authority we are given.

We have come to the point that what looks good to the eyes and what appeals to our senses, or whatever feeling we get during a church service is what God is all about.

When asked why people go to church in the first place, they say because it makes them feel good or they love the choir or adore the preacher. These are not reasons for establishing the "The House of Prayer."

We then go home and complain that our lives are destitute, our marriages are falling apart and sickness has ravaged our homes. We live in dysfunctional families where moral decay has been passed down through generations. We go to church, sing a few songs, have the preacher preach us happy and wonder why we don't encounter life changing results.

Through the endless cycle of giving without proper motive and being forced into obedience, we end up getting cursed because our agendas were not pure in the first place.

For some the church has become a place of promotion riddled with hidden agendas. It has become a place to promote concerts and musicians, all wanting to make a name for themselves. It has turned into a place where leaders have sold out to the people because the congregation has gotten bored with the entertainment value of the service.

Some go to church because it fits their lifestyle and what is preached is not difficult to apply, because no application is ever enforced in the minds of the congregants. They go to the church of convenience rather than where they can better themselves and get fed in order to sustain proper individual and spiritual growth.

Like the man who looks in the mirror and forgets what he sees, there are Esau's in the world that attend church on a regular basis. They receive what makes them feel good and then when the realization comes into being of what they have actually lost, they blame someone other than themselves.

God's voice has been shut up in churches and in some places, He is not present at all. When the leader starts to submit to the followers, we end up with Adam once again in the garden. When the preacher ends up selling out to his congregants, then we see Esau come back to life again.

The endless cycle and lifeless living without the power of God being manifested in the church, is one of the reasons why the world is in the chaos that it is.

There is anger and protest about homosexuality in the world and people will yell, argue and even picket for this particular cause. What I don't see are people who are picketing for the other sins in the world. Why are there no demonstrations against lying, cheating, adultery, murder, slander, abuse, disobedient children, and general lawlessness? Why are we distracted by one sin, when we should be living according to all of what God says and not just by listening to a few who are not listening to God in the first place?

We have bowed down to what has made the loudest noise, because we don't want to deal with it. The world has created a fear to speak out about what God says and in response the church individually and corporately, bows down to what Satan deems as moral.

Sin is sin. It makes no difference to God what it looks like or how we try to rationalize it, to make it fit our own personal lives. Now I know that the homosexual individuals will want to come out and attack me and

I wouldn't expect anything less. I will however stand my ground and lump it in with all the other sins that have infected and manifested themselves in the generations that are here at present.

God didn't create homosexuals, liars, cheaters, adulterers or murders and all the other myriads that sin has built. He did however allow everyone a way out of temptation and gave us the choice of what we are to do. Nothing has changed from God's original intention. The fight between God and Satan is still going on, but now Satan knows that his time is short.

God loves all of sinners, regardless of which one you are rallying for. That is what the cross was for in the first place. Each time we sell out to what makes us feel good or what we ourselves see as correct behavior, we are right back in the garden having a conversation with a serpent instead of listening to God. The more time we converse with the world, the less time we converse with God.

We are not able to fully function when half of us are in the world's way of doing things, and the other half is one step short of heaven. No amount of altar calls will remedy a quick fix to the situation. It's time to get real with what is real. It's time to be true to whom God made you to be and not your own personal idea of what truth is. There is only one author of true truth and that is God.

He is God and He sent His Son to hang on a cross for every one of us. Whether you are a liar, cheater, homosexual or adulterer or whichever sin you keep as a pet; He loves us all. If anyone has a problem with that, they ought to take it before God.

Our problem is that we want what God wants to give us, plus what we ourselves want for us. We want the easy way that feels good with no corrective measures in place. We want our world to change but we don't want to do anything to change it. We want God to be Santa Claus or a genie where we can give some money and poof, we get our wish.

We have gotten so off track from what God really wants for His people. We don't even know what He looks like anymore, because there are not many examples willing to speak up and just be who He has created them to be. We have become a people who are afraid to call it as God calls it out of fear that it might hurt someone's feelings. Since when does God say, let your emotions control you?

We have been taught by dubious preachers and teachers what God looks like. We have entertained false doctrine in regards to postions in churches and made them into stage acts where people receive glory. WE have prophets who are not prophets, apostles who are not apostles and preachers who are self appointed. When did God die and leave man in charge to rewrite the rules of the Kingdom of God? We have lost the way and now we don't even know what the model of Christ the Church even looks like. When it does show up, our senses are so dulled and fleshy, that we don't realize the Kingdom for what it is.

People say they love God and I believe they do. I'm just wondering what their god looks like, because they certainly don't look like the one I read about in the gospels. We are constantly trying to figure Him out instead of searching Him out. We rationalize logically when His ways are not our ways and His thoughts are not our thoughts. It is great to know that the Lord is still sovereign however and He will see that His chosen people will see Him for who He really is.

It is now that He will bring the world low so that His people will be seen rising up. They will be the ones with the answers. They will be the ones that will be full of His genuine power while exercising what the Word says. They will look like God, talk like God and walk like God. Their only agenda will be God's agenda. They will be the ones that God has raised up for such a time as this. They are the ones that God will use to bring order to the chaos that exists.

The world we see today is without form. The worldly structures are being torn down and will soon be replaced with God's New World of Order. He will bring a change to Sunday morning, because right now it is not how God intended it to be. We have used it as a place to bring our problems of the moment. Like spiritual junkies, we go in and get a fix and feel better about our situation without any real change taking place. Then when it's all over, we forget God and go back to what got us there in the first place.

Satan is so active in this politically correct world. We place limits on God's Word, because preaching it the way God said to preach it brings controversy. They twist the righteous Word of God into the perception of hate, thus bringing fear upon those who really want to do what God says to do.

Certain churches give God a bad name by preaching fire and brimstone, combined with harsh judgments and condemnation filled hate and lack of hope.

Don't get me wrong, God does discipline, but Jesus came to die for our sins when we don't always get it right. The church is supposed to be the moral authority, but most have crossed the lines of proper behavior and exhibit actions that are not conducive with His Image of Royal Decorum.

We sellout as Esau did because it gives us a sense of power and prestige. We figure we are untouchable because after all we are in the House of God. What we don't realize is that we are made even more accountable for our actions than if we had never been there. We believe that our good deeds will get us into heaven. We throw out the verse of "faith without works is dead," and replace it with "I'm a nice person and I do good things. That's good enough."

We start to think that we can do whatever we want because God forgives anyway. We believe the lie and then wonder why nothing in God is panning out the way we want it to. We start to give up on God because He isn't doing what we thought He said He would do. Eventually we give up or throw a temper tantrum because God didn't bow down to our desires. Instead of us rising up to meet Him, we choose to believe and interact with a serpent instead of believing God.

We sell out our kingdom authority for a pair of shoes, or a new car that will eventually rust and be salvage for a junkyard. We give our rights over to a serpent that has messed with the Godhead and in a heavenly chess game wages us as his pawns. We sell out on our birthright, because it was given to us as a free gift. We don't understand the value of it, because Jesus had to give up and establish His, in order for us to have ours.

Esau didn't see how important his birthright was until it was taken away. He didn't see how important it was and the power it came with, because he didn't see the value. It came to him too easy. All he did to be able to receive it was be born into the world.

Jesus knew that His dying on the cross would produce the same thing. Birthrights and inheritance is free but it will cost the tests of faith. He allows us not to be tempted beyond what we can stand, because we have to learn the importance and power of our own birthright. Without it we would take it for granted.

We are taught that since Jesus died on the cross, we don't have to suffer. If we don't have to suffer, we do not receive the full appreciation of what our Father has done for us. This is why we must carry our own cross. We need to see what it feels like to carry someone else's problems instead of our own. We need to see what it feels like to live in someone else's shoes, so that we learn not to judge so hastily. We need to understand what all of us messed up people go through, so that we are able to judge with a discerning mirror in front of us. I have seen nowhere in the bible where it says that you will not suffer for the cause of Jesus. In fact it is quite the opposite.

Matthew 16:

You're not in the Driver's Seat

21–22 Then Jesus made it clear to his disciples that it was now necessary for him to go to Jerusalem, submit to an ordeal of suffering at the hands of the religious leaders, be killed, and then on the third day be raised up alive. Peter took him in hand, protesting, "Impossible, Master! That can never be!"

23But Jesus didn't swerve. "Peter, get out of my way. Satan, get lost. You have no idea how God works."

24–26 Then Jesus went to work on his disciples. "Anyone who intends to come with me has to let me lead. You're not in the driver's seat; I am. Don't run from suffering; embrace it. Follow me and I'll show you how. Self-help is no help at all. Self-sacrifice is the way, my way, to finding yourself, your true self. What kind of deal is it to get everything you want but lose yourself? What could you ever trade your soul for?

Don't ever let people tell you, that you must be doing something wrong, because you are suffering. The funny thing is, is that you can be in pain and they will not help you. In the pain however don't allow it to breathe doubt in whatever process God is working in you. They don't know the importance or value of Godly spiritual process.

Satan will make light of it and those who say that it isn't from God are no better than Satan for they are anti-Christ. They make a mess of their own lives and then will have the audacity to blame someone else for it. Many have sold their birthright and yet they will not take responsibility for the actions of why it was taken in the first place.

Jacob saw the value of a birthright. He knew what it was like to be second favorite to his Father. He knew what he wanted and he seized the moment when it was presented in front of him. This same Jacob was the same one that saw angels ascending and descending in the place where he rested. He laid his head upon "a rock" and he went after God. He witnessed the connection of how a birthright works, for now He was connected directly with heaven. Jacob wrestled with the angel and said that he would not let the angel go until he was blessed. He was fervent and fought for what was his. He was not about to let anyone steal away from what God wanted for him. He was an example of what it may take at times to rule in kingdom authority.

The world or Esau took for granted a gift that his father gave him. When you don't realize your position you will abuse your authority. You will listen to a voice that teases your ears and works on the empty parts of your life. This worldly or earthly voice will tell you what you want to hear instead of what you need to hear. It will make you feel good about yourself without the substance and foundation of process.

Satan uses trickery to disguise himself as an angel of light. We will be attracted to that same quality in him, if that is what we want others to see. The world wants to make ourselves look good without process, but God wants us to process so that He can look good through us.

We have to carry our cross, carry another's burdens and appreciate what Jesus did for us on a real level. These characteristics and qualities are therefore not taught but are learned through practical experience and coached with spiritual guidance, to keep us on track and in alignment with the purposes of God.

Issues With Our Bloodline

A Blood Issue

Contrary to popular belief, God does not have an issue with Man. Man has an issue with Him. What is this issue? It's an issue with sacrifice. It's an issue with man's heritage, genealogy or bloodline. It's an issue of blood.

It's an issue of our bloodline when Man was first created.

-Luke 8

As Jesus went, the people pressed around him. [43] And there was a woman who had had a discharge of blood for twelve years, and though she had spent all her living on physicians, she could not be healed by anyone. [44] She came up behind him and touched the fringe of his garment, and immediately her discharge of blood ceased. [45] And Jesus said, "Who was it that touched me?" When all denied it, Peter said, "Master, the crowds surround you and are pressing in on you!" [46] But Jesus said, "Someone touched me, for I perceive that power has gone out from me." [47] And when the woman saw that she was not hidden, she came trembling, and falling down before him declared in the presence of all the people why she had touched him, and how she had been immediately healed. [48] And he said to her, "Daughter, your faith has made you well; go in peace." [2]

---

[2] *The Holy Bible : English standard version.* 2001 (Lk 8:42–48). Wheaton: Standard Bible Society.

This woman represents Eve in the garden as well as the church. The number twelve represents the government of God which was upon Jesus shoulders when He was born into this world. The woman was bleeding, hemorrhaging in a place that was unclean to the world.

The fringe of His garment was bound by a blue cord that served to remind the wearer of God's commands and the need to obey them.

She knew the importance of adhering to the order and structure of God. She knew what it took to receive supernatural healing from the Throne of God. Therefore when the woman touched the hem of His garment, she already knew that that was where the authority and power was and anything that was unclean or not prospering in her life would be healed. She did not touch His hem in hopes to be healed; she touched it because she already knew what would happen when she came into agreement with it.

To "touch" something you come into or you are brought into mutual contact with the thing or person you are touching. When something is mutual, you are in agreement. You are in covenant.

She was just acting on what she already knew. Her mind, body and spirit were in sync and now she knew what she was supposed to do. Agreement made way for her life to line up the way God wanted. She knew that once she got into agreement with it, she would be able to operate in the same power that Jesus had.

Jesus knew someone had touched Him because it was so odd to have someone touch Him in that manner. It was then that she could no longer be hidden. Now His power was flowing through her. He came against her bloodline of Adam and Eve in the garden. Now her blood was replaced with His power.

She accepted the terms of the kingdom operation, when she touched His garment. She submitted herself to His authority and she tapped into the government and power of God.

In order for the woman to even have the understanding that she would be made well, she would have had to believe first and apply second. Without the application of actually touching Him, she would not have received the power to heal everything that was ailing her in her life.

When Jesus said "Who touched Me?" He wasn't asking because He didn't know. He was asking in the sense of "look at who touched me." He was giving His disciples a visual lesson on what happens when you come into agreement or operate in the government of God. He wanted them to see what it looked like when you tap into His Power. He traded the bloodline of Satan with the bloodline of God.

She had an issue of blood. Her issue tapped into the only bloodline that really mattered. Like an electrical plug looking for an energy source, you will not have the power until you are plugged into the right connection and in the proper way. Power flows when everything is alignment. If it's not shocking things result.

The bible says that no man could cure her, but agreement with God cured her. In a moment she regained not only her health but also her true identity. She was a son (daughter) operating in the rule and authority given to her and everything was now under her feet.

In correlation, most individuals have been bleeding and hemorrhaging in a way that no man can fix. Sin and decay have made them their home and congregations have been helpless. They have an issue. They don't know who they are. They don't know their position and they don't know how to come into agreement with what God or what He is saying. What they have been taught has now led them to distrust anyone trying to pour into them. They cry out for help and for God to come in order for their issues to be healed. They don't understand that it takes faith to act and it takes mutual contact or relationship with Him, for His power to react back.

Those outside the Kingdom are bleeding in a way that man finds difficult to bring relief or viable answers. The world is dying because it has listened to a serpent with a hidden agenda. People in the world are decaying because they believe that life will heal itself. Others will choose to ignore it in hopes that it will just go away. All the while the issue keeps bleeding. The church and God's people cry out that they want to be healed and God replies: 2 Chronicles 7:14 **"Then if my people who are called by my name will humble themselves and pray and seek my face and turn from their wicked ways, I will hear from heaven and will forgive their sins and restore their land"**

We believe that our own blood or our own sacrifice will heal our situations. If we drop more money in the bucket, God will show up. If we do some more good deeds, God will show up. If we sing songs and dance, God will show up. When we think like this we end up trying to bribe God instead of just believing what He said.

Her actions spoke. She didn't have to speak; she just needed to act in accordance to His Order and manner. She was healed because her faith was mutual with Jesus. She saw things the way that Jesus seen them. She felt things that Jesus felt and touched Him in the manner that was acceptable in His eyes. It is then that she tapped into His Power and the impossible became possible.

Kingdom Dynamics
Structure and Order of the Throne
The Kingdom of Our God

About Our King
The God of Order and Structure

God is eternal, all-present, all-knowing and all-powerful.

GOD is and he may be known. Since the existence of God is not subject to scientific proof, it must be a postulate of faith; and since God transcends all his creation, he can be known only in his self-revelation.

We live by His Book and His Word. The Bible or (code of conduct) is written not to prove that God is, but He reveals to us Who He is in his activities. For that reason, the biblical revelation of God is, in its nature, progressive. In the light of His self-revelation in the Scriptures, there are several fundamental affirmations that can be made about Him. We practice these affirmations on a daily basis for they are required to maintain our citizenship in His Kingdom.

He pervades everything, organic and inorganic, acting from within outwards, from the centre of every atom, and from the innermost springs of thought and life and feeling, in a continuous sequence of energizing effect.

He made the world and everything in it, the Lord of heaven and earth, and does not live in temples built by hands. And He is not served by human hands, as if He needs anything, because He himself gives all men life and breath and everything else. In Him we live and move and have our being.

As citizens we do nothing apart from Him, because we cannot do anything without Him. We would not be able to remain citizens of His kingdom, if we removed ourselves from His proclamations, decrees and His Sovereignty.

I. His Being

In his being God is self-existing. While his creation is dependent on him, He is utterly independent of the creation. He not only has life, but He is life to His universe, and has the source of that life within Himself.

God is independent of every environment in which He wills to make Himself known.

He is the everlasting God, the Creator of the ends of the earth. He will not grow tired or weary. He gives strength to the weary, and increases the power of the weak. He is the Giver, and all His creatures are receivers.

Christ Who is His Son, gave this mystery its clearest expression when he said 'For as the Father has life in Himself, so he has granted the Son also to have life in Himself' (Jn. 5:26).

This makes independence of life a distinctive quality of the Throne head. He is the Fountainhead of all there is, animate and inanimate, the Creator and life-giver, who alone has life within Himself.

In his nature God is pure Spirit and Truth and He communicates using the same mechanisms. Our respect of Him is through our everyday life. We show our appreciation for the breath of life in us, by communicating in the manner He has created and through His etiquette of which He wishes us to live. We don't wish to live improperly and insult Him. We don't wish to give Him a wrong or bad image, for that is disrespectful of being part of His Kingdom. Since love is one of the determining factors of everyday life in His kingdom, we choose to live the life; He has given to us, in order to extend His graciousness to others.

God is sovereign. He makes his own plans and carries them out in his own time and way. His sovereignty in willing and working is simply an expression of his supreme intelligence, power and wisdom. His Will is not arbitrary, but acts in complete harmony with His character.

The Bible teaches us that all life is lived in the sustaining will of God 'in whom we live and move and have our being', and that as a bird is free in the air, and a fish in the sea, so we humans have our own real freedom providing what we are doing is within the constitutional will of God. God sustains us all in the responsible freedom of being accountable to Him. We are able to choose what to do, within His freedoms, so that we are able to go delve into deeper freedoms. Without these freedoms,

living for Him in faith and love, we are able to enjoy Him as our supreme God and King, and also enjoy the rights and freedoms of living as one of His citizens.

God is essentially unlimited, and every element of his nature is infinite. God is eternal, all-present, all-knowing and all-powerful.

His infinity likewise means that God is *transcendent* over his universe. It emphasizes his distinctness as self-existing spirit, from all his creatures. He is not shut in by what we call nature, but infinitely exalted above it.

He does not stand apart from the world, a mere spectator of the work of his hands. He pervades everything, organic and inorganic, acting from within outwards, from the centre of every atom, and from the innermost springs of thought and life and feeling, in a continuous sequence of energizing effect.

God who made the world and everything in it, is the Lord of heaven and earth, and does not live in temples built by hands. And he is not served by human hands, as if he needed anything, because he himself gives all men life and breath and everything else', and then affirms his immanence as the one who 'is not far from each one of us, for "In him we live and move and have our being"' (Acts 17:24, 28).

III. His character

God is personal. When we say this we assert that God is rational, self-conscious and self-determining, an intelligent moral agent. As supreme mind he is the source of all rationality in the universe. Since God's rational creatures possess independent characters, God must be in possession of a character that is divine in both its transcendence and immanence.

GOD's names are to us the designation of his attributes, and it is significant that, historically, God's names were given in the context of his people's needs.

It would seem, therefore, more true to the biblical revelation to treat each attribute as a manifestation of God in the human situation that called it forth, compassion in the presence of misery, long-suffering in the presence of ill-desert, grace in the presence of guilt, mercy in the presence of penitence, and so forth, suggesting that the attributes of God designate a relation which he establishes with those who feel their need of him. That bears with it the undoubted truth that God, in the full plenitude of his nature, is in each of his attributes, so that there is never more of one attribute than of another, never more love than justice, or more mercy than righteousness, but that God is unchanging, undiminished and wholly involved in all that he does. If there is one attribute of God that can be recognized as all-comprehensive and all-pervading, it is his holiness, which must be predicated of all his attributes, holy love, holy compassion, holy wisdom, *etc.*

IV. His will

God is sovereign. That means that he makes his own plans and carries them out in his own time and way. His sovereignty in willing and working is simply an expression of his supreme intelligence, power and wisdom. God's will is not arbitrary, but acts in complete harmony with his character. It is the forth-putting of his power and goodness, and is thus the final determinant of all existence for the divine glory.

There is, however, a distinction between God's will which prescribes what *we* shall do, and his will which determines what *he* will do.

The sovereignty of God ensures that all will be overruled to serve his eternal purpose, and that ultimately Christ's petition, which his followers echo, 'Your will be done on earth as it is in heaven' (Mt. 6:10; 26:39–42) shall be answered.

It is true that we are not able to reconcile God's sovereignty and man's responsibility within a single logical frame. That is because we do not understand the full range of divine knowledge and comprehension of all the laws that govern human conduct. The Bible teaches us that all life is lived in the sustaining will of God 'in whom we live and move and have our being', and that as a bird is free in the air, and a fish in the sea, so we humans have our own real freedom in the will of God who created us for himself.

God sustains us all in the responsible freedom of being accountable to him for what we choose to do, and without this the deeper freedom of living for him in faith and love, and enjoying him as our supreme good, could not be.

V. His essential life

In his essential life God is a fellowship. The supreme revelation of God given in the Scriptures is that God's life is eternally within himself a loving fellowship of three equal and distinct persons, Father, Son and Spirit, and that in his relationship to his moral creatures God is extending to them the fellowship that is essentially his own

VI. His Fatherhood

The personal God can enter into personal relationships, and the closest and most tender that the Bible knows is that of Father. This was Christ's most common designation for the One to whom he prayed and of whom he taught, and in theology the name of Father is reserved specially for the first Person of the Trinity. There are four types of relationship in which the word 'Father' is applied to God in Scripture.

1. There is his *Creational Fatherhood*. The fundamental relationship of God to man, whom he made in his own image, finds its most full and fitting illustration in the natural relationship which involves the gift of life. Man is thus the counterpart of the general Fatherhood of God. Without the Creator-Father there would be no human race, no family of mankind at all.

2. There is the *Theocratic Fatherhood*. This is God's relationship to his covenant-people, Israel. In this, since it is a collective relationship that is indicated rather than a personal one, Israel, as covenant-people, was the child of God and she was challenged to recognize and respond to this fatherly relationship.

3. There is *Generative Fatherhood*. This belongs exclusively to the second Person of the Trinity, designated the Son of God, and the only begotten Son. It is, therefore, unique, and not to be applied to any mere creature. Christ, while on earth, spoke most frequently of this relationship which was peculiarly his. God was his Father by eternal generation, expressive of an essential and timeless relationship that transcends our comprehension.

4. There is also the *Adoptive Fatherhood*. This is the redeeming relationship that belongs to all believers, and in the context of redemption it is viewed from two aspects: that of their standing in Christ, and that of the regenerating work of the Holy Spirit in them. This relationship to God is basic for all believers, as Paul reminds the Galatians: 'For in Christ Jesus you are all sons of God, through faith' (Gal. 3:26). In this living union with Christ they are adopted into the family of God, and they become subjects of the

regenerative work of the Spirit that bestows upon them the nature of children: one is the objective aspect, the other the subjective. Because of their new standing (justification) and their relationship (adoption) to God the Father in Christ, they become partakers of the divine nature and are born into the family of God. And so they are granted all the privileges that belong to that filial relationship: 'if children, then heirs' is the sequence (Rom. 8:17).

It is clear that Christ's teaching on the Fatherhood of God restricts the relationship to his believing people. Nowhere is he reported as assuming this relationship to exist between God and unbelievers. Not only does he not give any hint of a redeeming Fatherhood of God towards all men, but he said pointedly to his fault finding opponents: 'You belong to your father, the devil' (Jn. 8:44).

While it is under this relationship of Father that brings out the tenderest aspects of God's character, his love, his faithfulness and his watchful care, it also brings out the responsibility of our having to show God the reverence, the trust and the loving obedience that children owe to a father. Christ has taught us to pray not simply 'Our Father', but 'Our Father who art in heaven', thus emanating reverence and humility.

However intimate, rich and warm-hearted is His love, God remains God, majestic, amazing and awesome.

About The Son of the King- Jesus the Christ

Jesus is Son of God who was given the title of distinction of "Christ" or "Anointed One". He was sent to earth as Jesus, with His Father's government upon His shoulders. The King consecrated Him and anointed Him to operate in His great redemptive work as Prophet, Priest and King of His People. He took on the assignment of carrying out the King's orders of restoring the nations of the earth back to His Father.

He came to earth to establish the rule and order of God's government in a visual way, where people could relate. He brought the governmental way of God to the earth and carried it upon His shoulders. He instituted us the Way, gave us the Truth of how heaven operates and the ability to be light so that we may live a life with purpose and order.

Upon His arrival on earth, He demonstrated to mankind, that though Satan may lie, cheat and threaten to kill you, he cannot win. He revealed his lies and showed us, how to how to walk in a state of miracles. He revealed how we can be like Him, if we follow what He said and in the order that He said it. He came to bring order to a world that was running out of hope. Through His Father consecrating Him by allowing Him to die on the cross, we then were able to look forward to Christ resurrecting in us, when our own flesh dies. Jesus showed the inhabitants of the earth that we are given dominion over this land and we are to start walking in what is given to us. Jesus was and is a gift from the Heavenly Monarchy. He came as a representative of the Father, our King.

He came to earth on the orders proclaimed by the King Himself. Jesus was instructed to fulfill those orders, as they were royal decrees set in place for the salvation and redemption of mankind. Those decrees were the King's Will. They were royal proclamations that were to be completed, so that He could reign as Christ, at the right hand of the Father.

He showed us the importance of following those decrees and the degree of seriousness involved. He brought forth to earth the government of the Kingdom of God. He brought forth the laws of heaven and what is required for citizenship. He came to show us who we were and who we are.

The King is so serious about His Kingdom rule, that His only Son died in order to establish it. He showed us that we cannot mix the world and its influences with kingdom etiquette and authority.

A kingdom without rules is anarchy. A kingdom without power is lawlessness. Jesus came to restore order in His people. He came to establish the church, built on the structure and commands of God. He is of God and Is God within Himself.

Isaiah 9: 6 For unto us a Child is born, Unto us a Son is given; And the government will be upon His shoulder. And His name will be called Wonderful, Counselor, Mighty God, Everlasting Father, Prince of Peace. Of the increase of *His* government and peace *There will be* no end, Upon the throne of David and over His kingdom, To order it and establish it with judgment and justice. From that time forward, even forever. The zeal of the Lord of hosts will perform this.

He is supreme. He is Alpha and Omega. He is roomy that everything of God finds its proper place in Him. Within Him are many places and within Him we each have a place. From beginning to end He's there, towering far above everything and everyone. So spacious is He, so roomy, that everything of God finds its proper place in Him without crowding. Not only that, but all the broken and dislocated pieces of the universe; people and things, animals and atoms; get properly fixed and fit together in vibrant harmonies.

He came to show us that we are not orphans in this land. He came to destroy the plans that Satan wants us to believe. He came to show us that we have someone we can connect with and truly understands our plight on earth. He is our friend for all eternity.

About His Holy Spirit
The Directive Office

His Holy Spirit has the ability to transcend time and space, while relating to our own specific personality. The fact that the Holy Spirit has a personality is proved from the fact that He possesses the attributes of a personality. He can be funny, joyful, sad, compassionate etc. He not only has a personality, but He also has intelligence and volition. He loves to reprove, help, glorify and intercede. His person and personality allow Him to execute the offices peculiar only to a person. The very nature of these offices involves personal distinction. His divinity is established from the fact that the names of God are ascribed to Him and divine attributes belong to him. He is omnipresent, omniscient, omnipotent, and eternal.

Creation is accredited to him as well as the working of miracles. He is able to relate to us in a way that we understand, while operating within the King's authority.

He is powerful and wonderful both at the same time. He is marvelous in all His Works. He is never late and always on time. He brings light to the Father. He reveals what the Father and the Son say and speak. He brings sight by revelation. His actions reveal the power of God in the earth. Without Him we would not have the chance to learn or be comforted. Without Him we would not be able to be approved citizens of His Kingdom.

He is the Spirit of the Living God. God is not complete without Him and Jesus, His Son. They do not live independently from one another, and they operate dependent on each other. You cannot just have one and not any other. If you reject One, then you reject them all. They work in conjunction with each other and provide a harmony that brings order out of chaos.

The Chain of Command

God's governmental system works through the following arrangement and procurement of power. God is order and God is a God of Order. When He selects a disciple who has reached his field or kingdom of operation, an order is sent out, so that His structure on the earth can be built. This structure is only revealed by God the King and Father first. When the order is issued the King knows what He wants built and sees the end result of what He has ordered to come forth.

When the order comes forth it has no specific guidelines, but a spiritual picture is drawn in the terms of how it is to be built. The King has given all Authority to His Son and therefore, because His Son has fought many battles and given His life, He entrusts Him with the same authority He has upon Himself. The King has anointed Him to do His work. Anointing is the power conferred to do as the King as spoken.

When Jesus the Prince receives this order from the King, He designs it with specifics on how it is to be built and releases the authorization for all the materials needed for the structure to be built. He will include visual diagrams and His divine instructions as to its length, breadth, width and height. It will include the foundation and the elements needed to endure and withstand all attacks against it. The structure will take shape in the manner and time that He has ordered.

When these directives have been commanded, they now go to the Office of Divine Directives, The Counselor, which is His Holy Spirit.

When the Holy Spirit receives the commands from The Commander, He issues directives and makes sure that the information given is released through the proper channels.

His Administration office is responsible for issuing the following directives in the manner and specifics that the Commander has given. These directives when issued are given in a timely manner and therefore must be obeyed by man when issuance is given. The Holy Spirit works in conjunction and harmony with the King and His Commander Jesus for the structure to be built in the appropriate time and season.

Any disobedience to the Holy Spirit therefore is considered high treason or a sin against His Majesty the King. Persons not carrying out the instructions in the directives, place themselves in a position of exclusion for entrance into the Kingdom of Heaven.

These are the following directives:

The Holy Spirit shall in the commanded and appointed times create and give life. He shall appoint and commission ministers. He shall direct each minister where to preach. He shall direct each minister where not to preach. He shall instruct ministers what to preach. He shall strive with sinners. He shall reprove. He shall comfort. He shall help with weaknesses. He shall teach. He shall guide. He shall sanctify. He shall testify of Christ. He shall glorify Christ. He has a power of His own. He shall search all things. He works according to His own will. He dwells with saints. He can be grieved. He can be vexed. He can be resisted. He can show Who He is and how much power He has, if provoked.

He is for the saints. He reveals the things of God. He reveals the things of Christ. He reveals the future. He brings the words of Christ to remembrance. He directs the way in godliness. He teaches saints to answer persecutors. He enables ministers to teach. He guides all into all truth. He directs the decisions of the church, both individually and corporately. He attends to instruction. He is not allowed to receive things of the natural man. He raises up and trains Truth disciples.

Seeing Into the Kingdom of God
From the Citizens in the Kingdom of God

Under the Sovereign reign and ruler ship of our God, He has given each citizen a scepter. This scepter is a scepter of justice and righteousness. We speak of glory in His Kingdom. Each of our generations speak, create and manifest His perpetual glory. Like a perpetual watch, glory is created by movement. The King speaks through His Son, which is given to the Holy Spirit and we in obedience manifest what was spoken by our King. What the King has spoken in one generation, another generation will manifest.

Perpetual motion is created by the constant action and results in His reaction in His citizens. We speak of His glory, because we are Glory Carriers. He fills us, so we can have the ability to produce thankfulness and therefore fill His Kingdom with His Glory.

The Kingdom of our God is not of food and drink, but of righteousness, peace and joy in the Holy Spirit. We do not serve a King who is full of political rhetoric and hot air, but we serve a King of power. We know His ways and His ways have power, for we are citizens with empowered lives. The kingdom of God we live in cannot be shaken, so therefore, we as citizens are thankful and we show our thanks by doing what He requires of us.

This is our worship, and we do this for Him with reverence and awe.

His Kingdom endures forever and from one generation to the next, our depth in Him grows. Therefore we are thankful for the generations placed before us, for God graced us with a sensitive springboard, which has the ability to propel us deeper in the knowledge and ways of Him.

Very limited access is available to those who wish to reap the benefits of citizenship in the Kingdom of God. The gate is very narrow. No flesh is allowed, for only Spirit and Truth reside here.

Flesh cannot hear our King for He only speaks in Spirit and Truth. Only those who know Him and those who hear and obey His Voice will understand. We as citizens are considered sheep, for He is our Shepherd and guides us into the way that we should go every minute of the day. We have One Shepherd and we know Him in the manner He speaks. Though some of us may hear Him audibly, others hear what He is saying when He speaks through His Word. Therefore, we are able to relate to what He is saying, in regards to our own personalities and growth in spiritual understanding.

> In order to be granted access here, we first had to become a disciple; a disciplined man or woman of the Most High God.

When we made the choice to become a disciple, the King's will for us began to manifest through the revelations of His Spirit. We then began to have an intimate knowledge of the mysteries of His Kingdom.

We as citizens can only express and lead by example the way to the King. In doing so, our very lives teach the ways of the Kingdom as we continue to model through His Son. We carry His love and we have become His love that is ever growing. Thus, we are love reciprocators with the Godhead; repeating the love that God so graciously gave to us.

We are honored to be a citizen in the Kingdom of God, by serving as a Kingdom of priests. We are regarded as the good seed of The King. For what we hear from His Word, we understand and the Lord multiplies the revelation, each time producing more glory for Him. As we partake more and more of His nature, we cannot help but shine in the Kingdom of our Father.

We are a city of citizens that shine like the sun, because His Glory cannot be contained. He takes us from glory to glory to glory and His heights are immeasurable.

We work in harmony with one another just as our Godhead works as one. Even our scribes take their orders and commands directly from the Throne as given by His Spirit. They bring in new gems of truth as well as the old.

Not everyone is married in the Kingdom of God. Some are not mature enough to live a married life. Marriage requires a certain aptitude and grace. It isn't for everyone. Some, from birth seemingly, never give marriage a thought. Others never get asked or accepted; while some others decide not to get married for kingdom reasons. However, if someone is capable of growing into the largeness of marriage, we are able to do it.

Before we were citizens we had to ask ourselves who would we rather be like. One who eats the dinner or one that serves it? In the midst of our asking the Lord intervened and took His place as One who serves.

We went through a lot of things while witnessing Him serve us. In the process we learned how serving was appropriately done. We had no idea that we had to become a disciple or disciplined man in order to walk in His heavenly perception. However, as we killed our flesh, His Spirit revealed to us our Father and in doing so, revealed who we really are.

It was then that He conferred on us His royal authority that our King bestowed on Him. Since this was done we are able to eat and drink at His table and we are strengthened as we meet with the many gatherings of His people.

Though it was and at times not easy, we have a partnership with our King. This partnership contains perseverance through trials and tribulation. Together we endure for the sake of the Kingdom. We protect the Gift that was given to us, knowing the cost of its redemption.

Rejection for protection comes with a promise from the King Himself. We are assured and reminded that we will not regret the sacrifices we had to make in order to follow our King. The Christ who is the Son of the King, assures us presently, that whatever we sacrificed including home, spouse, brothers and sisters, that all to this day will continue to come back multiplied. We never lose out! It comes back to us continually over our entire life. On top of that, we are also granted a bonus of eternal life.

We as citizens are spoiled like no natural parent could ever spoil us. Our King owns everything upon and in the earth. He has given us kingdoms under His to rule over in His name. We plant our stake in the ground and overcome the evil one, by claiming and taking all we see in His name.

Though we had to be crushed and broken for Him, we lost all of our earthly fleshly possessions, but we inherited His Kingdom. Though we were persecuted for searching for the righteousness of God, we endured and became His heir. We had to be led and disciplined by Jesus the Christ, our older Brother, who knows the way to our Father. We have learned to always let Him lead, and have learned from when we first lost sight of our Father.

We had to learn obedience as a child, because our King and Father only has children. We had to accept and believe that He had a place for us in His kingdom, because it was the only way we could redeem our reservation. We know how happy our Father is, when

He is able to give us a kingdom which was prepared for us before the foundation of the world.

This kingdom we rule under His authority consists of commanding and going forth in that which He requires us to possess. We do this to further expand His territory and to glorify Him through our many great and expansive exploits. For just as our Father conferred upon His Son a kingdom; so He does with us also.

We as citizens live our everyday life in accordance to the laws that govern the Kingdom of God. Some people think that the Kingdom of God does not have rules, obligations or responsibilities. However there would be no Kingdom if these were not in place. The kingdom of God would look like the kingdoms of the world and then there would be no need for the kingdom of heaven.

We understand that laws are required in order to rule. Where there is no rule there is no law. We know that our Father has given us grace to maintain our kingdom citizenship. We have the knowledge that the commands put forth, are to remind us of what we once were like. We also know that His grace covers us, should we mess up from time to time.

We don't however keep on sinning so that God can show us more of His wonderful grace. Of course not! Since we have died to sin, how could we possibly continue to live in it? We were joined with Christ in baptism. Not only the physical baptism of water immersion, but also baptized our flesh into His blood, by the surrendering of our lives to Him. Now just as Christ was raised from the dead by the glorious power of the Father, now we also live new lives.

We are united with Him in His death and we also have the assurance of being raised to life as He was. We know that our sinful selves were crucified with Christ, so that sin would lose its power over our lives. Now, we are no longer slaves to sin. When we died with Christ, we were set free from the power of sin. Therefore, since we died with Christ, we know we live with Him. Death no long has any power over Him and now neither over us. Through the process of killing our flesh, we became dead to the power of sin and alive to God through Jesus the Son.

We don't let sin control the way we live and we have learned how not to give in to our sinful desires. We do not let any part of our bodies become an instrument of evil in order to serve sin or its master. Instead, we give ourselves completely to God

continuously. We do not want the sin that was dead to come back to life. Now, since sin is not our master, we no longer live under the requirements of the law. Instead, we live under the freedom of God's grace. To live under the freedom of His grace however, we understand completely that we have to live a surrendered life daily, in order to operate in the rights and freedoms that have been granted to us.

Some state that they are able to do whatever they choose, because of the generous offer of grace that our Lord has given. Grace sets you free from the law, but the laws are still in effect. We choose to explain it in this manner.

When one breaks the law, that person goes to trial and is judged according to the actions that were made. Once judged the person is thrown in jail. He is under the law, and is confined so that he or she has learned the lesson from breaking it. However when the person comes out of the jail cell, it does not mean that the law is taken away. It simply means that now that he or she has learned the lesson, and now have repented, that law no longer has any effect on them. The law is still in operation, but since they are dead to that sin, it no longer is a jail cell to them.

Obedience in the law is a necessity for all of us in the Kingdom. We realize that we become a slave of whatever we choose to obey. We had to make a choice to be a slave to sin, which leads to death, or we can choose to obey God, which leads to right standing and right living with all the benefits attached.

We as citizens of the Kingdom have found the freedom we were looking for. We live in joy, peace and love. Our compassion grows daily. There is no need for titles here, for we lay down our crowns before the Throne on a daily basis.

We don't want glory, but we cannot help its radiant light that shines forth out of us. We are humbled to serve. As individual citizens, we are not here to preach anyone happy and we are not here to enable you to stay where you are. We are here to bring forth the Kingdom of God on the earth.

We hope you will join us soon.

What is the Kingdom of God Like?

For the Kingdom of God does not consist of eating and drinking, but of right conduct, peace and joy, through the Holy Spirit. It consists of those who have had God make their decisions in everyday life.

Its citizens consist of those who have turned from their friends, families, children, brothers and sisters and even their own life to follow the commands of the Father. Each has carried their own cross forsaking their past traditions and ungodly ways. These are those who base their life upon God, regardless of what anyone says or thinks. They place the Father as the head of their life and forsaken all else.

Kingdom citizens do not need a preacher to tell them what they have already sought God after. They are the ones that have lived rejection to its ultimate. They are the ones hated by the world, because they believe God's word. This is not to be confused with those who dislike certain personalities or traits; it is the hate that comes from them just being themselves, even when they do not speak. They are rejected because the Son was also rejected.

Citizens are true disciples and bear the witness of God's power within them. They are humble, not showy, gentle and nature and often forgot about in the world. Citizens are not self centered, but are accused constantly of wrongdoing even if there is no evidence of such accusations.

They have weighed in their minds to follow the King on purpose. They do not just claim to follow because it is expected of them, or because it's the trendy thing to do. They follow because of their deep love and commitment to Christ. They follow in response to being thankful and submit themselves daily to His purging, so that He can be greater in them. In this way, they pick up their cross daily.

They do this not to be showy, but to keep themselves humble before God and others, so that they remain the valuable citizens that they are. They may not scream and shout, they may not say anything, for they have the quiet confidence in Christ. Their quietness is only because they are listening to what God has to say next. They understand that God searches the heart and not outer appearances.

He searches for those after His heart and character, looking for those in whom He can impart His power and authority. Citizens will possess these attributes, because they are the signs of the mind of a true believer.

Christ declared forth the great commission and citizens of the Kingdom make those words manifest into reality.

Kingdom citizens are world changers. They don't all go to "church" for they are the church. They don't need someone to excite them because God excites them. They don't need a word, because they know they are a prophetic word spoken by God at their earthly creation. They are God's word made manifest, so that He Himself can be seen by others. This glory stands as a witness to His power and perpetual motion of the Godhead.

Kingdom citizens have weighed the consequences of following the world and have made the determination to follow Christ. They are those who have made up their minds to forsake everything they have and own in return for life of Christ. They do this in order to grasp the reason why they were created in the first place; to possess that which possessed them first.

They are salt. They are seasoned individuals who cause the heavenly food to be ingested to come to life. They give spiritual food flavor with just a dash here and a dash there and here a little and there a little.

They understand that any food given by the Father at times can be hard to ingest, so added salt makes it go down a whole lot easier. This is unlike the lot of the food that is out there nowadays.

Citizens are concerned when the food being fed goes down extremely easy. The food eaten is usually thrown out in one way or another, because it was bland and/or just wasn't digested. Those who eat this food tend to end up spiritually underweight and powerless. Rather kingdom citizens are so overflowing in the Spirit of the Living God that they manifest miracles, signs and wonders as they go out and preach the Gospel of the Kingdom.

They do not speak anything else, because they know that God did not commission them to do such things. They speak one sermon and the one sermon is about the Kingdom of God. They know what God has done for them and in the manner He has done those things.

They know that if they preach the Gospel of the Kingdom, everything else will come into alignment with what He promised. They understand that anything else preached away from what they were given authority to preach, is disobedience to the Father and considered high treason against the Throne.

They know they have authority only in the areas God has given them authority. This authorization of power only comes from the King. They realize they have no authority in any other areas except within their boundaries. These boundaries have been taught to them. They have learned what is permitted to do and not do, for these are engrained in their hearts and minds. They know what to allow and what not to allow. They make conscience decisions every moment of the day. Their Father is always in focus in all they do. They do not preach sermons for they are sermons. They live in a constant state of forgiveness, for they understand that not all come to Christ at the same time. They do not judge because they can relate to where those who are just entering have been. Though those in the kingdom are not perfect within themselves, they are transparent. With wisdom they will allow other to read their lives. They are living epistles for all to read.

They study to show themselves approved. This means they study the deeper things of God which help maintain their citizenship. They also do this so to be more acquainted with the Father and His ways and keep themselves teachable. They may not write books or preach on the street or church, but they have the knowledge and wisdom of Christ, that no one can dispute.

Their faith is like a mustard seed. When God gives the command, they go and do without questions, and rely on the fact that their King has the inability to lure them into a situation they cannot withstand.

They do His commands instantly upon hearing. Each time they have done so in obedience, their faith grows so large that it is a witness to everyone around them. Upon growth beauty and fruit are seen as a witness of God's faithfulness. They do not rely on their own understanding, but have the trust that if a command comes from God, it comes with a purpose of growth attached.

They do not look for appreciation that they fulfilled the will of God by others around them. They do because it is the expected behavior and proper etiquette in the Kingdom of God. They are familiar with the intimacy that comes from these commands and commune with Him daily as part of their saintly regimen.

They identify themselves with the Kingdom of God and fully comprehend that one cannot attain entrance into it by mere observation. They understand that just speaking or preaching, doing good deeds and trying to impress others with what it holds, does not validate citizenship. These are considered bystanders and they are not permitted in the Kingdom. It is only those that do the Word of God that are allowed.

They are not double minded. Their focus is on the King and they wait purposely on call to do His will and only His will. They are not double minded and have made up their minds to live in a state of surrender to God.

They know that they do not go to church or arenas to see the Kingdom, because it is neither here nor there. They understand it is within them.

They have witnessed many running after some who claim to have the power of God, but need the conjuring method in order for some manifestation to take place. They understand that God does not need conjuring. They know that God is within His citizens and when they show up, God has showed up already to relate to Himself.

Kingdom citizens love God in the way the King wants them to love Him. They are trees that are rooted in love. The Lord has revealed Himself to these, for they continually do His will and listen to do His commands. They have learned discipline. Their minds have been transformed and their service to the King is unparallel.

They are versed in the Kingdom's chain of command. They understand royal protocol and kingdom government with the weight it carries. They have studied Kingdom history and the passing of Kingly authority. They are cognizant of the responsibility of ruler ship because they have learned His way of ruling.

The King is able to trust them with the keys that have been passed down from the House of David. They comprehend the operational kingdom government of David. They know that it is only with this key that those in the generational line of Christ have access to its power. It is the only generational access pass that is able to open and close any door in the kingdom of Heaven.

They have the experience of opening the doors of the many mansions or places that the King has prepared. Just like the mustard seed, their faith grows when each door into a revelation brings them into something bigger than themselves. As each door opens new mysteries are revealed in the manner it is to be received.

The Kingdom of God is the place where God prepares you for the Kingdom of Heaven. "As it in heaven, so it is on earth."

The character of Christ that we are willing to aspire to have, is necessary to live in the Kingdom of Heaven. Our heavenly abode is no different from the life we are to learn on this earth from the One example set before us.

As we partake in the requirements in order to submit our flesh and replace it with the glory of Christ's body, we redeem our life coupon for redemption.

Christ died for all sin, but its kingdom citizens with the knowledge of this that greater responsibility is given. The gift of salvation is a free gift, but those in the kingdom understand that we must work with the gift that was given. Though the gift is free, they understand the lifelong cost it takes to remain in it's realm.

Part II

The Constitution of the Kingdom of God Acceptable Operations and Admission Requirements

Faith in the Constitution of God

Faith is the substance of things hoped for, and the evidence of things not seen.

How do I show evidence of what I believe? My actions testify to what I believe. Therefore what I believe is shown by what I do.

You are able to witness my belief, because I am able to provide you evidence of it. I have made a belief which is invisible now visible and have taken baby steps in the creative process.

We know what God the Father looks like, because of Jesus. Jesus said if you see Him you have seen the Father. He also said that He only does what the Father does. He made the invisible, visible!

He also said that He did not come to change the law, but to fulfill the law. When you fulfill it, you bring it to fruition. You submerge yourself in it. You become it. You are the embodiment of it. God gave the law, the boundaries to stay within in order to walk out what was necessary to fulfill the purpose that He has for you.

We adhere to heaven's constitution by submitting to the purpose for which we are designed. Staying in the constitutional boundaries, we are able to fulfill the law within that document.

In order to fulfill it, we must be in agreement with it. An agreement in biblical terms means covenant. A covenant is an agreement between two parties. You must be in agreement in order to begin to walk out the constitution. As in any constitution, provisions are made in regards to pitfalls and trials that one may encounter. As with the covenant, should we encounter any trials or downturns, God has provided provisions and a "way out."

We will not have knowledge of a "way-out" if we do not know what the terms of the constitution comprise. Therefore many die for lack of knowledge. If one does not abide by the boundaries or laws in the constitution, then you set yourself in a place of danger which is not good for you.

By abiding in the constitution you fulfill the constitution. If you abide by the agreement of rights and privileges, you are able to exercise those rights and privileges.

In biblical terms, Jesus came to fulfill the law and in doing so, fulfilled the constitution. By this process we are able to see Him, and additionally we also see our Father.

You cannot fulfill the constitution in spoken word only. In order to fulfill it you must do what's in it.

You cannot do it by repeating what someone else has told you about it. Each aspect must be experienced by the individual so that they in reality enjoy the privileges it has to offer.

You cannot fulfill the constitution if you only apply what is beneficial to you in a moment of weakness. You cannot trade or barter with any of its elements. Therefore "making deals" with the King is useless.

It is the law of the King. Within it holds His character. His character is Who He is. It is His code of conduct which is exercised in His authority. It is Him who is God who rules or one can ascertain "The Rule of God." His rule is His Word. His Word is a Sword. So those who live by the sword, die by the sword. His rule separates that which does not belong to His realm.

When we live by the constitution correctly, we are able to enjoy all the rights and privileges within it. In essence we are living by the sword because we are to live by its constitution. If we do not live by the constitution, then we reject it, and die because of our denial.

This heavenly covenant, agreement or constitution is for the empowerment of those entering and living within the Kingdom of God. Abiding by the covenant or agreement gives you access to the power and privileges that the King has in His kingdom. Therefore you become partakers of His kingdom.

Jesus fulfilled the rule, the rule of God's law; the heavenly constitution. He did not come to take it away but rather to fulfill it. In fulfilling it, He was able to show us the Father who we would not otherwise be able to see. He was able to demonstrate to us His supernatural power, because it is one of the privileged benefits we attain when we operate in the Kingdom of Heaven.

He confirmed the fulfillment by orally stating "it is finished." He was able to show His Father honor or (glory) by the ultimate fulfillment of the constitution.

Mathew 5- 17 "Do not think that I have come to abolish the Law or the Prophets; I have not come to abolish them but to fulfill them. [18] For truly I tell you, until heaven and earth disappear, not the smallest letter, not the least stroke of a pen, will by any means disappear from the Law until everything is accomplished.

Believe or Belief

You cannot believe in the constitution unless you act on what you believe. Being baptized is not just the identifying through an individual being submersed in water. It is the baptism of immersing yourself in Christ. Your entire being is in Him. Faith is only a portion of belief. Nothing you do is independent of Him. When you are submersed in water, you are taken over by that water. Just as with Christ, when you are submersed in Him, He takes over you, just as with water.

You cannot know what is in a constitution unless you have read it. You cannot enjoy the benefits unless you have believed in it. You cannot experience the reality of His kingdom unless you submit your entire self in His Rule.

Therefore the constitution of God is His Rule. He created it. He is it. He embodies it. To have the constitution of God, you must be the constitution of God and not a facsimile.

You just don't want to look, talk and walk like Him. You want to become His expression in the earth. You want to have His blood flowing through you, His feet walking in you and His mouth speaking out of you. You are not God, but you have the same constitution as Him.

You are proof that He lives. This proof validates that you are not a hypocrite. Those who are hypocrites only appear to have it. It is not engrained in them. It has not been sealed into their identity. Hypocrites have no power. They claim godliness but lack the power thereof.

What are Covenants?

Genesis 9:13

Then God spoke to Noah and his sons: "I'm setting up my covenant with you including your children who will come after you, along with everything alive around you—birds, farm animals, wild animals—that came out of the ship with you. I'm setting up my covenant with you that never again will everything living be destroyed by floodwaters; no, never again will a flood destroy the Earth."[3]

SATANS GREATEST FEAR IS NOT YOU LIVING FOR JESUS, BECAUSE EVERYONE BORN LIVES FOR HIM; FOR HE CREATED EVERYONE FOR HIMSELF. HIS GREATEST FEAR IS THAT YOU WILL LIVE IN HIM, THE WAY THAT HE LIVES IN YOU!

This bond or covenant gives us a complete circle. When we are wrapped up in the one another, there is no beginning and no end. It is a bond or eternity wrapped up in infinity. Satan cannot penetrate it because there is no entry. Furthermore, he has no keys to enter into to steal it's power and kingdom authority.

A covenant, when agreed upon, is a binding contract between two parties.

The corresponding word in the New Testament Greek is *diatheke*, which means "testament.". It is equivalent to the word berith in the Old Testament which means covenant.

Peterson, E. H. (2002). *The Message: The Bible in contemporary language* (Ge 9:8–11). Colorado Springs, Colo.: NavPress.

This word covenant is a compact between man and man or between tribes or nations. In entering into a covenant, Jehovah was solemnly called on to witness the transaction and hence it was called a "covenant of the Lord" The marriage compact is called "the covenant of God", because the marriage was made in God's name.

The word is used with reference to God's revelation of himself in the way of promise or of favor to men. Thus God's promise to Noah after the Flood is called a covenant. We have an account of God's covenant with Abraham (Gen. 17), of the covenant of the priesthood (Num. 25:12, 13); and of the covenant of Sinai (Ex. 34:27, 28); which was afterwards renewed at different times in the history of Israel.

In conformity with human custom, God's covenant is said to be confirmed with an oath (Deut. 4:31; Ps. 89:3), and to be accompanied by a sign (Gen. 9; 17). Therefore the covenant is called God's "counsel," "oath," "promise." God's covenant consists wholly in the bestowal of blessing (Jer. 31:33, 34).

A covenant of works is the constitution under which Adam was placed at his creation.

In this covenant, the contracting parties were God the moral Governor; and Adam, a free moral agent, and representative of all his natural posterity (Rom. 5:12–19). The promise was "life." Matt. 19:16, 17; The condition was perfect obedience to the law, the test in this case being abstaining from eating the fruit of the "tree of knowledge," etc. and the penalty was death (Gen. 2:16, 17).

This covenant is also called a covenant of nature, as made with man in his natural or unfallen state; a covenant of life, because "life" was the promise attached to obedience; and a legal covenant, because it demanded perfect obedience to the law.

The "tree of life" was the outward sign and seal of that life which was promised in the covenant, and hence it is usually called the seal of that covenant.

This covenant is abrogated under the gospel, inasmuch as Christ has fulfilled all its conditions in behalf of his people, and now offers salvation on the condition of faith. It is still in force, however, as it rests on the immutable justice of God, and is binding on all who have not fled to Christ and accepted his gift of salvation, which of course is righteousness.

A covenant of grace is the eternal plan of redemption entered into by the three persons of the Godhead, and carried out by them in its several parts. In it the Father represented the Godhead in its indivisible sovereignty, and the Son his people as their surety.

The conditions of this covenant were;

On the part of the Father

All needful preparation to the Son for the accomplishment of his work

Support in the work (Luke 22:43); and a glorious reward in the exaltation of Christ when his work was done (Phil. 2:6–11),

His investiture with universal dominion (John 5:22; Ps. 110:1); His having the administration of the covenant committed into his hands and in the final salvation of all his people

On the part of the Son the conditions were:

His becoming incarnate (Gal. 4:4, 5); and as the second Adam representing all his people, assuming their place and undertaking all their obligations under the violated covenant of works; obeying the law (Ps. 40:8; Isa. 42:21; John 9:4, 5),

Suffering its penalty (Isa. 53; 2 Cor. 5:21; Gal. 3:13), in their stead.

Christ, the mediator of, fulfils all its conditions in behalf of his people, and dispenses to them all its blessings. In Heb. 8:6; 9:15; 12:24, this title is given to Christ.

Therefore in order to receive the benefits of being in covenant both sides must come into an agreement to fulfill the terms.

Since a covenant is an alliance, compact and/or treaty the terms must be met in order to receive the benefits from being in the covenant itself. Jesus wants us to share in the cup of the new covenant.

He wants us to do as He did. He stated that since He was hated, we will be hated. Since He had to flee, we will have to flee. He said that if we wanted to follow in His footsteps we would have to suffer as He did.

From the perspective of covenant, we learn that His order is always in existence and is always working. There is no room for sin in His commands, for sin is what causes disorder in His kingdom.

Satan however has his own form of covenant and is rather seen as an alliance. Those who reject the righteousness of Christ and deny His work of salvation, then come into agreement or covenant with the works of Satan. This alliance is one that is exercised on those who prefer the operations in his kingdom as opposed to the Kingdom of God.

To do this Satan must lure, seduce, lie and trick his way into your everyday life, in order to form this covenantal partnership. His plans are to take you away from the cross and instill in you that it is not necessary that you follow the terms laid out in Christ's covenant with man. His plan is to twist the main focus of why Jesus came to earth and to take as many with him to his own demise, because he knows his time is short.

Those who do not study or have been lured into misunderstanding the Words of Jesus gospel and testament are especially at risk to his plans.

He already knows that we belong to Jesus, but he is looking for those who just know of Jesus sacrifice, but do not operate in the Kingdom the way Christ explained. He wants people to believe that they can do anything and still be accepted. If he can keep you away from the Truth and work on your carnal desires, then he has accomplished the task.

This demonic alliance is an agreement between two or more parties that rise up against those of God. The Lord said that he who is not for Him is against Him, for they are the ones of this covenant.

The terms of this covenant consist of laziness in the things of God in way He ordered them. These ego based mentalities fill one with pride, disorder and destruction of all types. It's contents promise life but are spoken against being agreement with God.

Basically anything that is not of God's Word in the manner it is to be taken, allows one to form a covenant or alliance with Satan and his angels. Satan promises instant gratification and God promises eternal life.

Satan wants you to believe you are free to do whatever you want with no ramifications. He wants you to believe that it doesn't matter what manifests in your life, it's all the same to God.

He wants you to believe that the term "God loves everyone and He doesn't make mistakes," and while this may be true, he cleverly leaves out mans responsibility out of the statement. He fails to tell you that "we as people make mistakes," but God doesn't.

After he has twisted these words, then he will further bring you down, by allowing you to feel that there is no hope, and that you may as well just give up.

This covenant or alliance with Satan, is ours by default if we do not accept Jesus sacrifice on the cross. In order to redeem the covenant of Jesus, we must operate within the constitutional confines in which makes us aware of how powerful we are against Satan's wiles. Without it, we allow ourselves to be lied to and tricked in to believing something that is not of God.

A covenant is a powerful thing. In it we can agree to become whatever is spelled out for us. Covenants are agreements of purpose. What we agree to is our own free will and decision.

We just have to make up our minds of whom do we want to give our loyalty and royalty.

The Constitution of God is the gospel's tool to help us make a decision which covenant we wish to belong. Though many believe they already have formed a covenant with God, most have made an alliance with Satan without even knowing.

In order to operate in any kingdom you must have agreements made with those in the realm. In this case it is either the kingdom of darkness or the kingdom of heaven. If we are lukewarm for God's Kingdom, He spews us out. Of course Satan is only too happy to welcome your residence into his kingdom.

Therefore, one's covenant with whomever they wish to serve is made in limited time on the earth. Regardless of which one is chosen, each individual will feel its effects for eternity.

The Entrance Requirements
For Kingdom of God, God's Seal
And Providential Power

The gate into the Kingdom is narrow and access into it is not easy. What denies you access, is the flesh. We must command our flesh to submit and die under the guidance and direction of His Holy Spirit. By allowing flesh to die, you are accepting Jesus sacrifice on the cross. It must be crucified and washed with the blood that Jesus offered you.

This is not the mere saying that Jesus died for my sin, but the process of denying what we want in replacement for what God desires.

Some may say, well we are under grace and yes we are under grace. This grace however is applied to help you endure the flesh killing process. We all know that you cannot pour new wine into an old wineskin. Why would anyone think that you can keep doing fleshly worldly things that reflect Satan, and still be part of the Kingdom of Heaven?

Grace is equal to the Holy Spirit saying to us: "I know you have given your life to Me. I know you have submitted to Me and through your submission, you may fall at times, but do not worry. When you fall, my grace is sufficient for you. But be careful not to jump instead of fall, because you do not want to be led into temptation. For to be led into temptation means that you are in disobedience, and in doing so, you provoke My judgment power."

We are to regard our fleshly life as a sinful life. We are to leave that life of death behind in order to enter into His Kingdom. If you constantly look back, you will be deemed not fit for the Kingdom of God. Looking back at the things we used to do, is an indicator that those things have not left you and that you continue to entertain temptation.

Moses Law or the law given to Moses is not the same as God's Law or the Law that is written in the hearts of His saved citizens. If we trivialize even the smallest item in God's law, God says we trivialize ourselves. We are to take His law seriously and show others the way, so that we can be found honorable in the Kingdom.

Unless one does far better than the Pharisees, in the matters of right living, they won't know the first thing about entering the kingdom of God.

Entering requires trust and submission through our thoughts, words and actions. These are the basics of character redevelopment. Satan the god of this world wants us to operate in a state of pride in what we do. He wants us to believe that we are who he says we are. He wants us to associate our works and materialism as standards for value and success. He wants us to rate our holiness by how important we are in our own minds. He wants our character to reflect his so that we will deny the gift of Christ sacrifice on the cross. God did not make us this way. We are to have the mind of Christ.

We are made in His image. We are a royal priesthood belonging to our Creator, the King of Kings and the Lord of Lords. We must authorize God to do a satanic character assassination within our minds. We must allow God to do what He must, in order to strip away those things that cause us to be unfit for the Kingdom. Why? Because the stripping process enables us be productive citizens in His daily operational agenda.

When the rich man asked what He must do to enter the Kingdom of God, Jesus responded to Him, by ordering him to sell everything He had and follow Him.

There are some that misread this and say that God wants you poor, in order to serve Him. Our God is a King. It makes no difference to Him whether you are rich or poor. He has the ability to make you rich or poor in a moment without your permission. He is not interested in material things, because He is Spirit.

Instead Christ was relaying to him, that he could not buy his way into the Kingdom. Also if he wanted to enter in, he would have to leave all the things that did not come from Him. Obedience and submission must be daily present. The rich man learned the world's way of getting rich, now he had to learn God's way of entering into the richness of His glory.

Entrance into the Kingdom causes future citizens to re-evaluate their own personal stances with God. Most of us grew up learning about God and how He operated through the ways of our fellow man. Ideologies were formed in churches, through family and/or friends. With these models in front of us, we took on or embodied the characteristics we thought looked like God.

Then we placed them on a mental platform or pedestal and placed an idealist spotlight on them. Some may have even positioned them in places where God Himself should have been positioned.

We only know God only through someone else that has spoken about Him to us. Since we have no other reference point, we end up trusting the human in front of us, instead of the One who placed him there. Then we get angry because he or she wasn't the person we had made them out to be. We actually and eventually found out that the person was human. We mistake grandeur and verbal eloquence as a sense of what empowerment looks like and consequently what God looks like.

God however is now replacing those things. He is leveling the playing field. It's time to grow up and be who he has called us to be. Not who we want or desire to be and not a title that we think we can earn.

He is first and foremost Who calls us to become like little children. He wants all to be teachable, full of wonderment and elemental. He wants everyone to return to square one and start over like little children, or lose the chance of even getting a look at the Kingdom, let alone get in.

If we become simple like a little child, God ranks us high in His Kingdom. We know that once we are like little children, we will be honoring God, because whoever receives us, receives Him.

When we are like children, God has His angels always in touch with the King, reporting back and forth to keep us in His hedge of protection. That is why those who bully or take advantage of us are disciplined by God's own hand. They will be considered as least among man in the Kingdom, for they will have no authority and their rank in the kingdom is useless.

On the other hand those who humble themselves like little children will be persons of eminence, full of virtue, authority and

power. They will be esteemed for their excellence and importance. They are the receivers of God's preeminent blessings. Their rank is high in the Kingdom of God.
How does one become like a little child?

Unless a person submits to His original Creator, the "wind hovering over the water" Creator, the invisible moving the visible, a baptism into a new life Creator, it's not possible to enter God's kingdom. When you enter into Him, He hides you!

When you look at a baby, it's just that; a body you can look at and touch. But the person who takes shape within is formed by something you cannot see and touch. It called the Spirit and it becomes a living spirit. When the wind blows no one knows where it came from or what direction it flows. All that is known is by what is seen. No one knows exactly when it started to blow and start moving things, but there is a witness to its moving.

Others are able to witness the Spirit moving in you, by the way you have changed and the person that you once were is no longer. This can apply two ways.

Others will know of what kingdom you belong, by your changed character. They will ask, what happened to you? You won't be able to pin it down exactly, but you will know that it has been there and the effects are seen. Others will see by your character, whether you worship in the Kingdom of Darkness or in the Kingdom of Heaven.

Therefore because of the enormity of personal responsibility, one cannot be reborn or birthed out of someone else's experience with God. There is no second hand information on how to do it. Every individual is a person, with a personal birth experience. This eliminates those who want to force themselves in. Their flesh is too big to enter through the kingdom's gates and Satan and his kingdom are not allowed in. The security gate at the kingdom's entrance has a key created especially for you. It is etched and designed with God's personal touch and imprinted with His character.

He took the time to write on the hearts of His kingdom citizens and we are sealed by the blood of the Lamb. In this manner we are able to experience the Father's home for us and not man's replicated version of it.

The King is sure of those who pretend know Him. These are those who have none of His wonder working power. They possess and operate in pride and judgment. Their foundation is based on their own version of human intelligence. These are those who would never feel the need to humble themselves. They serve within their self made timelines, rather than submit under God's timetable and in accordance to His commands. Their egos make it difficult for them to repent and cause humility to flow through their hearts.

Of course, no one that has been before God in sincerity humbleness and contriteness has ever been the same. He changes and transforms citizens minds back to where He originally created them. Upon restoration they are able to identify for themselves who is their Father and King.

Little children are always looking up, because of their natural height and stature. In the same way, we always look up to Him, for everything that we need. We are to be dependent on Him and commit our trust. In doing so, we align ourselves with His will so that we may receive the good things, that He so passionately wants to give.

In order to gain access into the Kingdom of God, His righteousness must also be sought. Some seek the Kingdom without righteousness. They wish to mix the kingdom of darkness with the kingdom of God.

However, we are to seek His kingdom and His righteousness.

The combination is the lock that reveals the kingdom rule of God. Those in the Kingdom, are citizens because they pursued the King and learned to be right standing in His Presence. Citizens are given the revelation of the mysteries of the Kingdom.

They live on the Word and the revelation in that Word. This revelation is given in order to validate the King's identity. We are to search with expectation and learn about being right standing with the King. Citizens do not determine the ways of the Kingdom of God; rather citizens are given grace to adhere to its requirements. Citizenship in the kingdom is one of submission and agreement with the Sovereign Throne of God. We cannot enter and tell the King how the kingdom works. The royal passport must include the terms of agreement or covenant with the Throne.

Acceptance of these terms, are necessary requirements for entry, because not everyone who calls upon the name of the Lord will enter the Kingdom. Knowing the correct password saying 'Master, Master,' for instance isn't going to get us anywhere with God. What is required is serious obedience by doing what the Father wills.

At the Final Judgment thousands will be strutting up to God saying, 'Master, we preached the Message, we bashed the demons, our God-sponsored projects had everyone talking.' He is going to reply to them saying "You missed the boat. All you did was use me to make yourselves important. You don't impress me one bit. Get away from Me."

Some think that the King's words are just incidental additions to a worldly life. They believe that they can apply a few words in the context of ideas, to make improvements in certain areas while disregarding the rest. They fail to believe that these words must be in operation and are needed for the foundational structure of the King to build upon. This foundation structure contains your destiny. It is the powerbase from where you build upon.

Many want to know what their purpose in life is. They want to know what God is saying in the moment, without even venturing into His word to find out for themselves. His Words are powerful. If we work these words into our lives, we are like smart carpenters who build houses on solid rock. These houses are strong and withstand the elements of the witchcraft of disobedience. They don't shift one day and another next. They are not built on slippery slopes.

But look!

Who are those who build their houses upon sand? These are those who can quote scripture to show others how self righteous they are. These are those who study theology to try to prove to others how they know all about God. These are those who use His words only in bible study and church. These are those who of one mentality one moment and another in a different moment. These are those who are without love, and will condemn and judge without looking in a mirror. These are those who cannot be taught, but yet believe they are wise. These are those who build their houses upon sand. Their houses that if once tested, would crumble, because a faith that cannot be tested cannot be trusted.

Satan's kingdom has taught the world that they will not have to suffer through any tribulations. His spirit has lied to them that if trouble hits their house, that God does not love them and is punishing them. However when storms do hit their lives, they are given the opportunity to examine the damage. They are able to see where reinforcing must take place. Through the trials and tribulations of life, Kingdom citizens are able to see how their houses hold up, and are there to help rebuild but on a new foundation.

Entrance into the Kingdom is limited and difficult. Access requires many tribulations and not just repetitive words. It takes love and willpower mixed with perseverance to get through. The love required is not love for what you want, but love for the desires of God in your life. Entry requires more than just listening to commands and orders, as some of these can be mistakenly heard on account of our own volition.

As a matter of fact, you will not be able to fully carry out His commands and orders, if your heart has no love for His kingdom and if your mind is bidding you to look backwards. When love and mind is misaligned, His commands become hindrances and His orders become jail cells filled with frustration.

That is why the greatest commandment in God's law is love. Without Him, you can do nothing. We have no chance at all if we think we can pull it off ourselves, but we have every chance in the world, if we allow God to transform our minds and bring us into His Kingdom. In doing so, we allow Him to be seen by others.

God is angry when we shut the door of the Kingdom of Heaven against men. We are to love our neighbor as ourselves and to be expressions of Him so that others will gain the benefit. How can we say we love our neighbor and keep the riches of His kingdom to ourselves? How can we love our neighbor if what we teach is not what God is saying, but is our own rendition of what we perceive Him to be?

Perception is not Truth.

Therefore Truth must be sought out. Truth is a priority. We are to acknowledge that God is number one. We are to love the Lord God with all our passions, prayer, intelligence and energy.

The second command is to love others as well as we love ourselves. No other commands outrank these. The rule of God is filled in the rule of His love. This does not nullify all the other commandments, but rather sets them in the proper order. Acknowledging and living in these, places you not only in Kingdom of God, but the King will place His seal on your character and you will identified as one of His own.

You will have the authority and power to operate in what you were destined for. You will naturally acknowledge His power, because it will be working in you and for you, while coming against all the things that come against the Throne of the King.

This is preparation for the sealing of God's people that He spoke of in the Book of Revelation. You can Be the Cause for Christ or you can Be As the Cause for Christ. If you are not for Him, you are against Him. If you are for Him you are His "BE" Cause. You are "BE"ing. who He designed and created you to BE.

If you are against Him, you deny His power and thus live a hypocritical life. Since you cannot BE His cause, you can only "Be As The Cause". This means that you can only make it look like you are for Him. Those who do this, deny the power of God in their lives by taking the glory for themselves. After all, you cannot give glory to something that you have taken already upon yourself. In these moments, these individuals operate in another kingdom.

This anti kingdom is also known as the kingdom of darkness. Those in this kingdom submit to its authority. They want the power of the kingdom of God, but do not want the discipline process which teaches how to operate in that power. They can only be as Him, for appearance sake. This is in opposition to being in Him, because to be in Him takes submission.

So we can become the "Jesus' cause" or" be as the cause"; Two definitions, two different outcomes. One spells life and the other spells death.

Be the "Jesus Cause"= JC or
BeAsThe Cause
One spells Jesus Christ the other spells Beast

Signs of Who Truly Believe

So that you will believe in the power and authority of the King in the people surrounding you, these are the signs of those who believe.

Signs of Those Who Believe (Mark 16:17-20)

[17] And these signs will follow those who believe: In My name they will cast out demons; they will speak with new tongues; [18] they will take up serpents; and if they drink anything deadly, it will by no means hurt them; they will lay hands on the sick, and they will recover."

Then the disciples went out and preached everywhere, and the Lord worked with them and confirmed his word by the signs that accompanied it.

**Remember Who You Are
And Whose You Are**

Elements of the Theocratic Constitution

You are ambassadors of the Kingdom of God. Anyone who does not believe in by acting or doing the rules of law that constitute the Will of the Father, will not enjoy all the rights and privileges therein.

BE IT KNOWN THAT THESE ARE THE CUSTOMS OF THE
CITIZENS IN THE HOLY CITY IN THE KINGDOM OF GOD.

THESE ARE THE DETAILS WHICH HIS MAJESTY OFFERS
YOU TO OPERATE IN, AS HIS STANDARD.

THESE ARE THE CUSTOMS IN THE
KINGDOM OF GOD AND OF HIS PEOPLE.
THIS GOOD NEWS IS TO BE LEARNED AND REINVESTED INTO
OTHERS, IN ORDER TO FULFILL
THE GREAT COMMISSION AND ALSO
GAIN AND MAINTAIN RESIDENCE IN HIS KINGDOM.
THEY ARE WHAT IS NECESSARY EXPERIENCES THAT BRING
ORDER TO LIVES AND TO LIVE COMFORTABLY IN THE PRESENCE

OF THE FATHER WHILE
RULING IN THE WILL OF GOD.
THESE LAWS AND STATUTES WERE WRITTEN BY HIS MAJESTY
IN THE FULLNESS OF HIS POWER AND GRACE
AND CHISELED INTO ROCK, WHICH IS HIS SON JESUS,
AND WILL LAST FOREVERMORE.

THESE COMMANDS ARE GIVEN BY GOD'S MIGHTY HAND FOR
PLACEMENT UPON HIS PEOPLE.
THEY ARE SET FORTH, SO THAT ALL WILL KNOW WHAT SIN IS;
FOR WITHOUT THE KNOWLEDGE OF THESE THINGS, ALL WOULD
PERISH.
THEY ARE FURTHER WRITTEN ON THE KING'S SERVANTS
HEARTS AND MINDS.
THEY WILL BE VERIFIED AND VALIDATED
UPON KING'S WILL,
THEIR CHARACTER AND IDENTITY WITH THE KING WILL BE
SEALED FOR THE PURPOSES OF THE LAST DAYS,
SO THAT THEY WILL ALWAYS KNOW THAT THE LORD, IS THE
LORD THEIR GOD FOR NOW AND ALWAYS!

The Kingdom's Constitution
For the Rule of God
For the Character of God
The Constitutional Covenant
Between
Man and God

Moral Laws and Prophetic Statutes
Declarations and Proclamations
Rights and Responsibilities

COMMANDS NECESSARY FOR THE OPERATION OF SPIRITUAL AND MORAL LIVING

IT IS WRITTEN IN:

PROCLAMATION OF GENESIS BOOK 20 ARTICLES 1-17

²I am the Lord your God, Who has brought you out of the land of Egypt, out of the house of bondage.

³You shall have no other gods before or besides Me.

⁴You shall not make yourself any graven image [to worship it] or any likeness of anything that is in the heavens above, or that is in the earth beneath, or that is in the water under the earth;

⁵You shall not bow down yourself to them or serve them; for I the Lord your God am a jealous God, visiting the iniquity of the fathers upon the children to the third and fourth generation of those who hate Me,

⁶But showing mercy and steadfast love to a thousand generations of those who love Me and keep My commandments.

⁷You shall not use or repeat the name of the Lord your God in vain [that is, lightly or frivolously, in false affirmations or

profanely]; for the Lord will not hold him guiltless who takes His name in vain.

⁸[Earnestly] remember the Sabbath day, to keep it holy (withdrawn from common employment and dedicated to God).

⁹Six days you shall labor and do all your work,

¹⁰But the seventh day is a Sabbath to the Lord your God; in it you shall not do any work, you, or your son, your daughter, your manservant, your maidservant, your domestic animals, or the sojourner within your gates.

¹¹For in six days the Lord made the heavens and the earth, the sea, and all that is in them, and rested the seventh day. That is why the Lord blessed the Sabbath day and hallowed it [set it apart for His purposes].

¹²Regard (treat with honor, due obedience, and courtesy) your father and mother, that your days may be long in the land the Lord your God gives you.

¹³You shall not commit murder.

¹⁴You shall not commit adultery.

¹⁵You shall not steal.

¹⁶You shall not witness falsely against your neighbor.

[17]You shall not covet your neighbor's house, your neighbor's wife, or his manservant, or his maidservant, or his ox, or his donkey, or anything that is your neighbor's.

KINGDOM ENTRANCE AMENDMENTS

THE GATE IS NARROW
NOT ALL WHO SAY LORD, LORD SHALL ENTER THE KINGDOM

KINGDOM ENTRY RESPONSIBILITES, BENEFITS AND TERMS

THE FOLLOWING ARE WHAT IS NECESSARY TO LEARN KINGDOM PRACTICES AND PROCEDURES.

THE INDIVIDUAL MUST SUBMIT THEMSELVES, IN ORDER TO RETRIEVE THE KEYS OF OPERATION THAT ARE REQUIRED FOR YOUR DIVINELY ASSIGNED LIFE TASK.

THEY ARE THE TEACHING OF THE APPROPRIATE USE OF POWER AND PROVIDE THE REVELATION OF HOW TO RULE IN THAT POWER.

UPON THE KING'S APPROVAL, YOU WILL HAVE THE OPPORTUNITY TO SHARE IN HIS GLORY, INCLUDING, RULING POWER IN YOUR DESTINED APPOINTMENT.

THE DESTINED APPOINTMENT IS THROUGH THE AUTHORITY OF THE KING. THEY ARE HIS PURPOSE FOR YOU AND WHAT YOU WERE CREATED TO DO UPON THE EARTH.

ALL LEVELS ARE REQUIRED TO BE ATTEMPTED THROUGH THE HELP HIS MAJESTY'S ANGEL ARMIES FOR YOUR PROMOTION AND STATUS IN THE KINGDOM OF HEAVEN.

IT IS UNDERSTOOD THAT EACH RESPONSIBILITY OR PROCESS THAT AN INDIVIDUAL EXPERIENCES WILL NOT BE ABOVE WHAT THEY CAN HANDLE MENTALLY, PHYSICALLY OR EMOTIONALLY. THEY ARE IN EFFECT TILL THE COMING OF OUR LORD AND SAVIOR JESUS CHRIST FOR THE PURPOSE OF PERFECTING HIS SAINTS FOR HIS GLORY.

Declaration of Foundational Scripture: Matthew 5:1-12

And seeing the multitudes, He went up on a mountain, and when He was seated His disciples came to Him. ² Then He opened His mouth and taught them, saying:

3 "Blessed *are* the poor in spirit,
   For theirs is the kingdom of heaven.
4 Blessed *are* those who mourn,
   For they shall be comforted.
5 Blessed *are* the meek,
   For they shall inherit the earth.
6 Blessed *are* those who hunger and thirst for righteousness,
   For they shall be filled.
7 Blessed *are* the merciful,
   For they shall obtain mercy.
8 Blessed *are* the pure in heart,
   For they shall see God.
9 Blessed *are* the peacemakers,
   For they shall be called sons of God.
10 Blessed are those who are persecuted for righteousness' sake,
   For theirs is the kingdom of heaven.

11 "Blessed are you when they revile and persecute you, and say all kinds of evil against you falsely for My sake. ¹² Rejoice and be exceedingly glad, for great *is* your reward in heaven, for so they persecuted the prophets who were before you."[4]

---

[4] *The New King James Version.* 1982 (Mt 5:1–12). Nashville: Thomas Nelson.

RESPONSIBILITY STATUTE I

Foundational Scripture-Matthew 5-3 3

"Blessed *are* the poor in spirit,

    For theirs is the kingdom of heaven.

YOU (INDIVIDUAL PERSONS) ARE THE CHURCH
YOU MUST BE POOR IN SPIRIT
THE INDIVIDUAL MUST BE POOR
IN THE SENSE AS IT PERTAINING TO THEIR SPIRIT

Protocol of Process for Covenant Acceptance

What it really means:

They must be willing to be destitute of the wealth of logical learning and intellectual culture which schools can afford. Man of this class readily give themselves up to Christ's teaching and prove themselves fitted to lay hold of the heavenly treasure, which is Christ Himself.

- In order to attain the Kingdom of Heaven, Man must be willing to give up his personal and carnal authority

- His flesh must come under the subjection and authority of His Majesty's Holy Spirit.

- He must be willing to lose worldly prosperity, influence and earthly stature.

-He must be willing to allow his flesh to perish, so that his Majesty's Divine Nature may shine through his earthly body.

-He must be willing to be removed from the power of death and not return to the kingdom of darkness.

-He must prostrate himself in spirit by submitting all earthly desires to the power of His Majesty's Divine Influence

-Complete submission and trust is absolute and necessary.

-He must be willing to endure the circumstances that God dictates. Sacrifices of one's own accord will not be accepted.

-Those who process in this manner shall be granted the Kingdom of Heaven.

RESPONSIBILITY STATUTE II

Foundational Scripture-Mathew 5-4 4

Blessed *are* those who mourn,
> For they shall be comforted.

MUST EXPERIENCE BEING MOURNFUL
Protocol of Process for Covenant Acceptance

What it really means:

Those who are mournful are sorrowful.

Must be willing to experience the sorrows that come with the separation of the **things of the world** they love.

Must be willing to mourn things that are no longer closest to them

Must be willing to replace their sorrow of earthly things for the things of His Majesty God

These are summoned to be comforted and are granted the assurance they will be comforted, by whatever means the Holy Spirit deems appropriate.

These individuals will be strengthened, exhorted and consoled.

In their consolation, they will be instructed and taught in how to be strengthened in their spirit according to His Majesty's service.

They shall love the Lord their God with all their heart, all their soul and all their strength.

They shall not have any other gods before the one and only eternal God, the creator of the heavens, the earth, and the springs of water.

RESONSIBILITY STATUTE III

Foundational Scripture-Matthew 5-5 [5]

Blessed *are* the meek,

For they shall inherit the earth

MEEKNESS
MUST BE MEEK TOWARD GOD IN THE DISPOSITION OF ONE'S SPIRIT, WHEN ACCEPTING HIS MAJESTY'S DEALINGS WITH MAN AS GOOD.

Protocol of Process for Covenant Acceptance

What it really means:

-These individuals must be willing endure trials and tests of faith without disputing, arguing or resisting.

-They must be willing to rely on God rather for strength, rather than their own to defend them against injustice.

-They must be willing to have experiential knowledge of meekness towards evil people. They are to know and understand that God is permitting the injuries they inflict and that He is using them to purify them, His elect.

-They must be willing to allow God to deliver them in His time. -

Those who are meek will receive a part of His Majesty's inheritance, thus they become an heir and they will receive their allotted possession by right of son ship.

-This inheritance is received through established meekness and as approved by God while being exercised in faith and abiding in love.

-Meekness is established by the rule of being broken in spirit and rewarded with a portion of His allotted Divine Inheritance.

RESPONSIBILITY STATUTE IV

Foundational Scripture-Matthew 5-6

6 Blessed *are* those who hunger and thirst for righteousness,
For they shall be filled.

You must hunger and thirst for righteousness
Protocol of Process for Covenant Acceptance

What it really means:

-Individuals must be willing to crave ardently and seek with eagerly desire the things by which the soul is refreshed, supported and strengthened.

-They must be willing to eagerly long for right standing with God - They must be willing to crave right standing with God and the human condition that is acceptable to God.

-They must be willing to exercise the doctrine that is approved by God

-They must be willing to forget carnality and walk upright, righteous and virtuous

-They must be willing to forget carnality and walk upright, righteous and with virtue.

-They must be willing to keep the commands of God

-They must be willing not pride his self in being righteous

-They must be willing not pride himself in his virtues whether real or imagined.

-They must be willing to accept Christ as his sacrifice in order to be held innocent, faultless and guiltless

-They must be willing to conform to the will of God

-They must be willing to not pass judgment on others whether expressed in words or shown in any manner.

-Their life must give evidence of what the King looks like and He must show this evidence by words and by allowing His life to teach.

-They must be willing to live the evidence of Christ in them, in order to give the evidence or proof of the fact thereof.

Responsibility Statute V

Foundational Scripture –Matthew: 5-7
7 Blessed *are* the merciful,
    For they shall obtain mercy.

Must Be Merciful
Protocol of Process for Covenant Acceptance

What it really means:

-Individuals must be willing to have mercy, seek mercy and give mercy.

-They must be willing to give mercy to those who are afflicted or seeking aid.

-Individuals must be willing to bring help to the wretched for in doing so, they will experience mercy

-They must be willing to actively seek mercy when afflicted so that others will be able to exercise the mercy that has been placed upon them.

-Individuals must be willing to have mercy when they live in a constant state of being merciful

Responsibility Statute VI

Foundational Scripture Matthew 5-8
8 Blessed *are* the pure in heart,
    For they shall see God.

Must Be Pure In Heart
Protocol of Process for Covenant Acceptance

What it really means:

-Individuals will see His Majesty when they have been purified by fiery trials through and from the permission and power of the Holy Spirit.

-These individuals will resemble a vine being cleansed by pruning so that they will be able to bear fruit.

-Their pure heart will be free from corrupt desire, sin and guilt.

-They will free themselves from every admixture of what is not truth and will be sincere and genuine.

-By accepting Christ's sacrifice on the cross they will be seen blameless and innocent. They will be unstained with the guilt of anything.

-Their heart will contain the Majesty's will and character and they will acknowledge it as the center of their spiritual life, through their evidence of their inner and outer life.

-Their pure heart will contain the will and character of God.

-Their mind which is the seat of their thoughts, passions, desires, appetites, affections, purposes and endeavors, will be those of His Majesty.

Responsibility Statute VII

Foundational Scripture-Mathew 7

9 Blessed *are* the peacemakers,
> For they shall be called sons of God.

Must Be a Peacemaker
Protocol of Process for Covenant Acceptance

What it really means:

-Those who love peace will make, produce, construct, form and fashion the road of God.

-They must be willing to be authors to the cause of Christ.

-They must be willing spiritual authors and declare the will of God in the earth.

-They must be willing to make ready, prepare, produce and shoot forth the purposes of God.

-They must be willing to lead those in bondage out of captivity

-They must be willing to carry out and execute the Word of His Majesty

-They must be willing to appoint and ordain the things of God.

-They must be willing to perform the promises of God

-They must be willing to command and order the declaration of the Lord

-They must be willing to call out and utter the Words of the Lord to exercise His Majesty's kingdom on earth.

-They must be willing to be called sons of God, for they revere God as their Father.

-They must be willing to have the character and life, are the arks that carry God, for they are governed by the Spirit of God

-They must be willing to have a calm and joyful trust in God, such as is children with their parents

-They must be willing to wear this dignity as sons of God

-They must be willing to spend affectionate intimacy with His Supreme Love

They must be willing and obedient to the Father's will in all His acts.

Responsibility Statute 8

Foundational Scripture 5

10 Blessed are those who are persecuted for righteousness' sake,
> For theirs is the kingdom of heaven.

Must be persecuted for because of righteousness

Protocol of Process for Covenant Acceptance

What it really means:

-Must be willing who suffer persecution because of His Majesty - These must be willing to be mistreated on account of His Majesty working in them

-These are those who are mistreated on account of their continual submission to Him

-These must be willing to be harassed, troubled and/or spiritually molested by those against the Throne of God.

-These must be willing to be pursued because of their love of His Majesty; for their enemies are hostile towards the King's Will and omnipresence.

-These must be willing to be persecuted because of their integrity, virtue, purity of life, right standing, and correctness of thinking, feeling and acting.

-These individuals are granted royal power, kingship with dominion and rule

-These have the right and the authority to rule over an assigned territory that is subject to the rule of His Majesty.

-These will rule in the Kingdom of Heaven.

-These individuals will have the right to rule in the authority of God, in the realm of His Kingdom. He will rule in the authority of God over all things that pertain to God and His Kingdom. He will not be God, but will represent the King in all His authority and will lead the people with signs and wonders which will accompany them.

-Their counsel shall come from the Trinity of His Majesty, The Godhead.

-These are those who are His Vice-regents, His magistrates and judges who rule in the order and in the things of God.

-Be it known to all under the sovereignty of our Lord, that when fulfilling the law, as Jesus the Son of God has done and has overcome; that you are to be blessed by command when people insult you, persecute you and falsely say all kinds of evil against you, because of His Majesty the King.

REJOICE AND BE GLAD BECAUSE YOUR REWARD IS GREAT IN HEAVEN, FOR IN THE SAME WAY THEY PERSECUTED THE PROPHETS WHO WERE BEFORE YOU.

Guaranteed Rights When Fulfilling Your Responsibilities In the Kingdom of God

Promises while fulfilling the Responsibility Statutes, So that the power of His grace will abound in you.

2 Corinthians 12:9 But he said to me, "My grace is sufficient for you, for my power is made perfect in weakness." Therefore I will boast all the more gladly about my weaknesses, so that Christ's power may rest on me.

Philippians 1:6 And I am certain that God, who began the good work within you, will continue his work until it is finally finished on the day when Christ Jesus returns.

Corinthians 1:8 He will keep you strong to the end, so that you will be blameless on the day of our Lord Jesus Christ.

Philippians 1:10 so that you may be able to discern what is best and may be pure and blameless until the day of Christ,

Philippians 2:12 Therefore, my dear friends, as you have always obeyed--not only in my presence, but now much more in my absence--continue to work out your salvation with fear and trembling,

Philippians 2:16 as you hold out the word of life--in order that I may boast on the day of Christ that I did not run or labor for nothing.

All of these contain master keys in the kingdom of God which open doors in the kingdom of heaven which usher you into the throne room or the kingdom of God.

Benefits of Fulfilling Your Responsibilities
The honor of being a Disciple of Christ
Eternal Life

The Right to Rule

A guaranteed place in the Kingdom of Heaven
The honor to serve your King
Power of a true believer

Victorious in all you do

Angelic Protection to fulfill your responsibilities
Granted a scepter of righteousness

Sealed and Validated as God's own. These who submit themselves to the Power and Authority in the responsibilities set forth, their acceptance of the process shall be considered those who have redeemed and accepted the sacrifice of Jesus upon the Cross. Therefore they shall be considered in covenant with the Lord Thy God. These shall also be considered of those who do the Word of the Lord when requested and required.

Those who do not do the Word of the Lord and blaspheme the Holy Spirit, the Kingdom of God shall be taken away from them.

Matthew 21:43 I tell you, the Kingdom of God will be taken away from you and given to a nation that will produce the proper fruit.[5]

They who adhere and submit in love to the responsibilities set forth, are be covered by His grace, for His grace is made perfect in

---

[5] Tyndale House Publishers. (2007). *Holy Bible : New Living Translation.* (3rd ed.) (Mt 21:43). Carol Stream, IL: Tyndale House Publishers.

their weakness. They shall be fortunate, blessed and happy, because these were especially chosen to fulfill these responsibilities.

Understand that this is the way in the Kingdom of God. Its responsibilities are necessary for pulling down strong holds and for mighty victories in Christ. They will remain continual until the day of His coming; the coming of our Lord Jesus Christ.

The Fulfillment of the Law

[19] Therefore anyone who sets aside one of the least of these commands and teaches others accordingly will be called least in the kingdom of heaven, but whoever practices and teaches these commands will be called great in the kingdom of heaven. [20] For I tell you that unless your righteousness surpasses that of the Pharisees and the teachers of the law, you will certainly not enter the kingdom of heaven.

KINGDOM OF PRIESTS-

THE ROYAL NATION-A HOLY PRIESTHOOD
PROPER BEHAVIOR IN THE HOLY CITY
HOW IT OPERATES

KINGDOM PROTOCOL FOR EVERYDAY LIFE
FOUNDATIONAL SCRIPTURE Matthew 5:21–8:1

RESPONSIBILITIES CONCERNING MURDER

"You're familiar with the command to the ancients, 'Do not murder.' I'm telling you that anyone who is so

much as angry with a brother or sister is guilty of murder. Carelessly call a brother 'idiot!' and you just might

find yourself hauled into court. Thoughtlessly yell 'stupid!' at a sister and you are on the brink of hellfire. The simple moral fact is that words kill.

"This is how I want you to conduct yourself in these matters. If you enter your place of worship and, about to make an offering, you suddenly remember a grudge a friend has against you, abandon your offering, leave immediately, go to this friend and make things right. Then and only then, come back and work things out with God.

"Or say you're out on the street and an old enemy accosts you. Don't lose a minute. Make the first move; make things right with him.

After all, if you leave the first move to him, knowing his track record, you're likely to end up in court, maybe even jail. If that happens, you won't get out without a stiff fine.

Responsibilities concerning Adultery and Divorce

"You know the next commandment pretty well, too: 'Don't go to bed with another's spouse.' But don't think you've preserved your virtue simply by staying out of bed. Your heart can be corrupted by lust even quicker than your body. Those leering looks you think nobody notices—they also corrupt.

"Let's not pretend this is easier than it really is. If you want to live a morally pure life, here's what you have to do: You have to blind your right eye the moment you catch it in a lustful leer. You have to choose to live one-eyed or else be dumped on a moral trash pile. And you have to chop off your right hand the moment you notice it raised threateningly. It's better a bloody stump than your entire being discarded for good in the dump.

"Remember the Scripture that says, 'Whoever divorces his wife, let him do it legally, giving her divorce papers and her legal rights'? Too many of you are using that as a cover for selfishness and whim, pretending to be righteous just because you are 'legal.' Please, no more pretending. If you divorce your wife, you're responsible for making her an adulteress (unless she has already made herself that by sexual promiscuity). And if you marry such a divorced adulteress, you're automatically an adulterer yourself. You can't use legal cover to mask a moral failure.

Responsibilities concerning Empty Promises

"And don't say anything you don't mean. This counsel is embedded deep in our traditions. You only make things worse when you lay down a smoke screen of pious talk, saying, 'I'll pray for you,' and never doing it, or saying, 'God be with you,' and not meaning it. You don't make your words true by embellishing them with religious lace. In making your speech sound more religious, it becomes less true. Just say 'yes' and 'no.' When you manipulate words to get your own way, you go wrong.

Responsibilities concerning Loving Your Enemies

"Here's another old saying that deserves a second look: 'Eye for eye, tooth for tooth.' Is that going to get us anywhere? Here's what I propose: 'Don't hit back at all.' If someone strikes you, stand there and take it. If someone drags you into court and sues for the shirt off your back, gift-wrap your best coat and make a present of it. And if someone takes unfair advantage of you, use the occasion to practice the servant life. No more tit-for-tat stuff. Live generously.

"You're familiar with the old written law, 'Love your friend,' and its unwritten companion, 'Hate your enemy.' I'm challenging that. I'm telling you to love your enemies. Let them bring out the best in you, not the worst. When someone gives you a hard time, respond with the energies of prayer, for then you are working out of your true selves, your God-created selves. This is what God does. He gives his best—the sun to warm and the rain to nourish—to everyone, regardless: the good and bad, the nice and nasty. If all you do is love the lovable, do you expect a bonus? Anybody can do that. If you simply say hello to those who greet you, do you expect a medal? Any run-of-the-mill sinner does that.

"In a word, what I'm saying is, Grow up. You're kingdom subjects. Now live like it. Live out your God-created identity. Live generously and graciously toward others, the way God lives toward you."

Responsibilities concerning attention getting

"Be especially careful when you are trying to be good so that you don't make a performance out of it. It might be good theater, but the God who made you won't be applauding.

"When you do something for someone else, don't call attention to yourself. You've seen them in action, I'm sure—'playactors' I call them—treating prayer meeting and street corner alike as a stage, acting compassionate as long as someone is watching, playing to the crowds. They get applause, true, but that's all they get. When you help someone out, don't think about how it looks. Just do it—quietly and unobtrusively. That is the way your God, who conceived you in love, working behind the scenes, helps you out.

Responsibilities concerning Prayer

"And when you come before God, don't turn that into a theatrical production either. All these people making a regular show out of their prayers, hoping for stardom! Do you think God sits in a box seat?

"Here's what I want you to do: Find a quiet, secluded place so you won't be tempted to role-play before God. Just be there as simply and honestly as you can manage. The focus will shift from you to God, and you will begin to sense his grace.

"The world is full of so-called prayer warriors who are prayer-ignorant. They're full of formulas and programs and advice, peddling techniques for getting what you want from God. Don't fall for that nonsense. This is your Father you are dealing with, and he knows better than you what you need. With a God like this loving you, you can pray very simply. Like this:

Our Father in heaven, Hallowed be Your name. Your kingdom come. Your will be done On earth as it is in heaven .Give us this day our daily bread. And forgive us our debts, As we forgive our debtors. And do not lead us into temptation, But deliver us from the evil one. For Yours is the kingdom and the power and the glory forever. Amen.

"In prayer there is a connection between what God does and what you do. You can't get forgiveness from God, for instance, without also forgiving others. If you refuse to do your part, you cut yourself off from God's part.

"When you practice some appetite-denying discipline to better concentrate on God, don't make a production out of it. It might turn you into a small-time celebrity but it won't make you a saint. If you 'go into training' inwardly, act normal outwardly. Shampoo and comb your hair, brush your teeth, wash your face. God doesn't require attention-getting devices. He won't overlook what you are doing; he'll reward you well.

Responsibilities concerning A Life of God-Worship

"Don't hoard treasure down here where it gets eaten by moths and corroded by rust or—worse!—stolen by burglars. Stockpile treasure in heaven, where it's safe from moth and rust and burglars. It's obvious, isn't it? The place where your treasure is, is the place you will most want to be, and end up being.

"Your eyes are windows into your body. If you open your eyes wide in wonder and belief, your body fills up with light. If you live squinty-eyed in greed and distrust, your body is a dank cellar. If you pull the blinds on your windows, what a dark life you will have!

"You can't worship two gods at once. Loving one god, you'll end up hating the other. Adoration of one feeds contempt for the other. You can't worship God and Money both.

"If you decide for God, living a life of God-worship, it follows that you don't fuss about what's on the table at mealtimes or whether the clothes in your closet are in fashion. There is far more to your life than the food you put in your stomach, more to your outer appearance than the clothes you hang on your body. Look at the birds, free and unfettered, not tied down to a job description, careless in the care of God. And you count far more to him than birds.

"Has anyone by fussing in front of the mirror ever gotten taller by so much as an inch? All this time and money wasted on fashion—do you think it makes that much difference? Instead of looking at the fashions, walk out into the fields and look at the wildflowers. They never primp or shop, but have you ever seen color and design quite like it? The ten best-dressed men and women in the country look shabby alongside them.

"If God gives such attention to the appearance of wildflowers—most of which are never even seen—don't you think he'll attend to you, take pride in you, do his best for you? What I'm trying to do here is to get you to relax, to not be so preoccupied with getting, so you can respond to God's giving. People who don't know God and the way he works fuss over these things, but you know both God and how he works. Steep your life in God-reality, God-initiative, God-provisions. Don't worry about missing out. You'll find all your everyday human concerns will be met.

"Give your entire attention to what God is doing right now, and don't get worked up about what may or may not happen tomorrow. God will help you deal with whatever hard things come up when the time comes.

Responsibilities concerning Behavior

"Don't pick on people, jump on their failures, and criticize their faults— unless, of course, you want the same treatment. That critical spirit has a way of boomeranging. It's easy to see a smudge on your neighbor's face and be oblivious to the ugly sneer on your own. Do you have the nerve to say, 'Let me wash your face for you,' when your own face is distorted by contempt? It's this whole traveling road-show mentality all over again, playing a holier-than-thou part instead of just living your part. Wipe that ugly sneer off your own face, and you might be fit to offer a washcloth to your neighbor.

"Don't be flip with the sacred. Banter and silliness give no honor to God. Don't reduce holy mysteries to slogans. In trying to be relevant, you're only being cute and inviting sacrilege.

"Don't bargain with God. Be direct. Ask for what you need. This isn't a cat-and-mouse, hide-and-seek game we're in. If your child asks for bread, do you trick him with sawdust? If he asks for fish, do you scare him with a live snake on his plate? As bad as you are, you wouldn't think of such a thing. You're at least decent to your own children. So don't you think the God who conceived you in love will be even better?

"Here is a simple, rule-of-thumb guide for behavior: Ask yourself what you want people to do for you, then grab the initiative and do it for them. Add up God's Law and Prophets and this is what you get.

Being and Doing

"Don't look for shortcuts to God. The market is flooded with surefire, easygoing formulas for a successful life that can be practiced in your spare time. Don't fall for that stuff, even though crowds of people do. The way to life—to God!—is vigorous and requires total attention.

"Be wary of false preachers who smile a lot, dripping with practiced sincerity. Chances are they are out to rip you off some way or other. Don't be impressed with charisma; look for character. Who preachers are is the main thing, not what they say. A genuine leader will never exploit your emotions or your pocketbook. These diseased trees with their bad apples are going to be chopped down and burned.

"Knowing the correct password—saying 'Master, Master,' for instance—isn't going to get you anywhere with me. What is required is serious obedience—doing what my Father wills. I can see it now—at the Final Judgment thousands strutting up to me and saying, 'Master, we preached the Message, we bashed the demons, our God-sponsored projects had everyone talking.' And do you know what I am going to say? 'You missed the boat. All you did was use me to make yourselves important. You don't impress me one bit. You're out of here.'

"These words I speak to you are not incidental additions to your life, homeowner improvements to your standard of living. They are foundational words, words to build a life on. If you work these words into your life, you are like a smart carpenter who built his house on solid rock. Rain poured down, the river flooded, a tornado hit—but nothing moved that house. It was fixed to the rock.

"But if you just use my words in Bible studies and don't work them into your life, you are like a stupid carpenter who built his house on the sandy beach. When a storm rolled in and the waves came up, it collapsed like a house of cards."

When Jesus concluded his address, the crowd burst into applause. They had never heard teaching like this. It was apparent that he was living everything he was saying—quite a contrast to their religion teachers! This was the best teaching they had ever heard.

RESPONSIBILITIES REGARDING FALSE PROPHETS

[15] "Watch out for false prophets. They come to you in sheep's clothing, but inwardly they are ferocious wolves. [16] By their fruit you will recognize them. Do people pick grapes from thornbushes, or figs from thistles? [17] Likewise, every good tree bears good fruit, but a bad tree bears bad fruit. [18] A good tree cannot bear bad fruit, and a bad tree cannot bear good fruit. [19] Every tree that does not bear good fruit is cut down and thrown into the fire. [20] Thus, by their fruit you will recognize them.

True and False Disciples

[21] "Not everyone who says to me, 'Lord, Lord,' will enter the kingdom of heaven, but only the one who does the will of my Father who

is in heaven. ²² Many will say to me on that day, 'Lord, Lord, did we not prophesy in your name and in your name drive out demons and in your name perform many miracles?' ²³ Then I will tell them plainly, 'I never knew you. Away from me, you evildoers!'

The Wise and Foolish Builders

²⁴ "Therefore everyone who hears these words of mine and puts them into practice is like a wise man who built his house on the rock. ²⁵ The rain came down, the streams rose, and the winds blew and beat against that house; yet it did not fall, because it had its foundation on the rock. ²⁶ But everyone who hears these words of mine and does not put them into practice is like a foolish man who built his house on sand. ²⁷ The rain came down, the streams rose, and the winds blew and beat against that house, and it fell with a great crash."

Of course anyone who puts these words into action must have faith. Faith is the action of God. Faith is an action verb. Hope is movement. Hope pulls you forward. You cannot have one without the other. You cannot have hope if there is nothing to believe in.

Faith and hope interlock with each other. Faith and hope are evidence that you believe that certain things will come to a particular end.

When the disciples asked the Lord to increase their faith, Jesus replied that if they had faith the size of a mustard seed it would grow. Jesus used a parable to describe the kingdom of God.

You can have faith and not use it. We are not to use it as a noun but as a verb.

The kingdom of God flourishes on a level that is not familiar with human common sense. This Kingdom is within each one of us and is not visibly seen. It is not heaven. It is a realm where royal protocol is an absolute. Not everyone has the appropriate key for entry. In order to enter, you must be in agreement with God and submit to His Authority or His way of doing things. Just as David sought God and asked Him to teach him His ways, so we must do also. His Kingdom has no end, so therefore we must remain teachable and not hard hearted or set in our own ways. We must be willing to cast away old traditions and religious mindsets that may be passed down from former generations that do not line up with the Kingdom of God.

The gospel of the kingdom is not what most people think. The gospel of the Kingdom is the good news of the kingdom. Its good news is that once we are in agreement with heaven, we will learn and understand our heavenly heritage and in the process receive the revelation of its operating procedures.

The Two Kingdoms
Kingdom of God vs Kingdom of Darkness

There are two systems on planet earth that are exercised through the thoughts and behavior of mankind. Whether we like it or not we are placed on this earth to delegate the things of God by whom all things were created.

The first system is the Kingdom system that Jesus taught when upon the earth.

This kingdom system empowers human behavior through the act of change and repentance. This brings about a transformation in the human mind which reflects in ones' thoughts and subsequent actions. It is a system that Jesus came to this earth to show, model and reveal to us. He modeled what is required to operate in it. He came to give us a representation of what our Father requires of us in order to manifest Christ in us.

It is one where outsiders can see what we believe by how we live and the power that is exercised through us when are in alignment with Him. It is a system that reveals who and how powerful Christ is in the individual that operates through Him.

It is a system that requires all aspects of our human experience. It is a system that requires submission through the giving over of our thoughts, actions, desires and behaviors in order to attain the power that can only come from the heavenly throne. On earth Jesus amplified the human experience and taught us how powerful we too can become. When operating in it through submission to Him, it cannot help but be accompanied with signs, wonders and miracles. The Kingdom System is the perfect model for proper behavior. It is Christ's perfect structure and example of how we are to live. It is filled with the spiritual influence and guidance of the Holy Spirit and is one where order and authority establishes itself on the foundation of God's Word.

God who is sovereign upon the earth maintains the order of the humans that He has created. He created each with their specific purpose and has organized strategies for a completed assignment.

He established the "house of prayer" from where His order would come forth. He has spoken directly to those have been entrusted by His hand. Each finger on His hand represents the fivefold ministry gifts of God for His people to be enabled and provided with the proper tools necessary for the saints of the most high to rise up and possess the kingdom. This kingdom system is one of order.

It is one where God our Father sits on His Throne with Jesus our brother by His side, watching who of His creation is modeling His behavior. This system is one where we are asked to be partakers of its movement, but we are not forced to do so.

It is one where our love for God is paramount, regardless of the situations we walk through. It is a system that establishes itself, precept upon precept. It is one where a person's life does not only look like God, but also talks like Him, walks like Him, and exercises the same power and authority. It is a system where victory in God is not only possible but mandatory. It is an entity where God is revealed and not learned. It possesses and holds a spiritual architecture that blows the minds of logical people. It is more precious than gold and it cannot be torn down, manipulated or purchased through the greed of man.

Its system of hierarchy is backwards to the earthly mind, where the last will be first and the first will be last. It is a system that roots it's foundation through true relationship built upon Christ whom is the foundation. It is one where we don't have to be perfect, we just have to be in alignment. It is one where we allow ourselves to be the glove that covers His presence in us. It is one where when He moves, we move and when He talks, we talk.

The Kingdom of God is not a place, for Jesus said that it is not here nor there, but that it is within us.

More often than not, people are looking for a Kingdom that is a literal place and they confuse this place with heaven. Although heaven is the place where the Throne of Glory establishes Himself, it is the only place of authority where this system exerts its power over and through mankind.

In order to rule in this authority, we must first be renewed and changed. When in the process of this change we learn what God's Kingdom is really like and change our perception who really is our Father and Brother. Those who operate in this Kingdom system will exercise, practice and BE the Word of God, instead of those in the world system who talk about it.

This kingdom system is a threat to the world system. When it rises up in power, it comes with a standard that the world will attack. It is a system that is so powerful, that if it wasn't threatening, nothing would rise up to attack it. Those operating in it, are often under attack, just as Jesus was when He was here. Leaders in that day called Him crazy, a fanatic and a menace. Therefore those in the position of ruler ship, will be anyone from church leaders to those who are not yet in the public eye. They will be housewives, children, teenagers, church goers, teachers, preachers plus an entire range of those not mentioned. One thing is for certain all will be attacked and ridiculed in one form or another.

The rate of attack is thus in direct correlation to the nature of the kingdom's power working within the individual. People operating in the kingdom system are those whom the worldly religious system has rejected. This kingdom system is one that provides opened gates for the lost, depressed, persecuted and rejected. It is a system that defies human logic and worldly understanding. It is one where the revelation of God is in visual operation to those who live within it.

It is a movement where faith is offered up to be stretched and exercised. It is a place where God shows Himself in the individual first then allowing Himself to be seen to others around that same person. It is a system that is not built on rules but rather on principles that when operated produce great power, strength and determination.

Its doctrine is one where people become living epistles of God or living epistles of Satan. All will be read by what they believe. This system will be preached throughout the whole world. Jesus said, when the gospel or good news of the kingdom is preached throughout the world, and then the end would come. This gospel of the kingdom is to not be confused with the gospel of Jesus Christ. The gospel of Jesus Christ is the foundation for the gospel of the Kingdom.

The world's system is delegated with the concerns, answers and strategies given through the human perspective. They are brought forth through the twisting and misuse or inactive use of God's word in the earth realm. This system is one that misappropriates and misrepresents the order of God upon the earth. It is a system that claims to be God like, but its practices are the opposite of what the bible teaches. You cannot say you are with God and then believe the opposite. You cannot mix the world system with the kingdom system. They are at odds with one another. They are opposites. This then is to be viewed as anti or against Christ. This system is the majority of what is now being delegated throughout the earth. Keep in mind that this system is not a religion but a way of thinking. The world system has religiosity engrained within it to a point of condemnation and judgment. It constantly ridicules in a pious fashion in order to lift itself up and think highly of itself. It is the biggest and largest form of witchcraft in the world.

Merriam-Webster describes witchcraft as one of its definitions as
- an irresistible influence or fascination

It is a belief system that bewitches you with instant gratification, greed, corruption, selfishness and manipulation. It is cunning, perverted and it is in direct opposition to the Kingdom System.

It is chaotic and without form. It is filled with unruliness, contempt and is complemented with lack of discipline in the behavior of all who are in it. It is a system that validates and celebrates anything that is unholy. It is one that emphasizes non corrective behavior by making reasons and excuses to continue in it, instead of bringing the correction needed.

It blurs the minds of the people to thinking that they can never be more than they are and they can never do more than what they have been accustomed to. It is a system of laziness, where God is Santa Claus or a trained magician. It is a system that promotes greed in respect to "look at what I have" and get it through whatever means necessary. It is a system where your thoughts line up with what your hand does. People do what they believe. Whatever a man thinks so is he.

This Satanic system is a system where one can either go to church or say they love God by praying, singing, and dancing. They then go out and give a misrepresentation of who God by condemning, putting others down, gossiping and being mean to their fellow man.

These are those who go to church or believe in God for the wrong reasons. People in this spiritual structure will idolize the preacher, instead of God. When this is evident, when they find out their pastor isn't perfect, they accuse and attack instead of restoring as the bible says to do. These people will point out the sins of the leader, but will not look at their own. They are hypocritical in deeds and selfish in their needs.

These are those who go to church and use it as a business or pickup place or a place to show off the latest fashions. These are those who act as though they praise God and then go home and complain about what they don't have. These are those who have been in the church for years and live selfish, depleted lives wanting someone else to come worship them in their party of pity.

They will tell you about the goodness of God and be jealous of their neighbor in the following sentence. These are the ones that you will see every Sunday serving their god and then see them in a bar, totally intoxicated and be telling others how much they love God. People in this system don't believe that you should have to suffer for anything. They tell you that God's blessings are without sorrow. What they don't realize is that the blessing is in the sorrow.

It is a system where people mimic what is ungodly and proclaim godliness. It is hypocritical in nature and is opposed to the character and model of Jesus. Simply put, it is a system that talks about the Word of God, instead of being the Word of God.

It is a system that persecutes God's chosen people. It uses the term we all sin and not one of us is perfect as excuses to continue in sinful behavior. It categorizes sin in degrees when God sees sin in all the same degree.

This abomination causes the emptiness or desolation in the people of the earth. It places itself in a power position that it was not awarded. It causes death and emptiness to those who encounter it. It is the force of the Kingdom of Darkness that presents itself as a sacrifice on its own terms. It's theocratic terms are lies written in air that imitate and reason away the terms of Covenant of God. This kingdom that is establishing itself has the power of a beast. A beast eats flesh, lives on flesh and wishes all to do the same. It does not want you to deal with the spirit of God in you, because that is too powerful for it to handle. That is why it cannot allow anyone to BE the Christ in them; instead it wants them to Be As The Theocracy or Beast, if we were to abbreviate the term.

This beast takes power into its own hands in the Temple, just as King Uzziah did. Just as the church is individual and corporate, so is the bodily temple, both individual and corporate. This beast power wishes to take your Kingly power into his own hands and use your authority from God to rule over the Kingdom of God.

The only authority this beast has is the authority the individual gives it. The priests with King Uzziah did not authorize him to do what he wanted in the temple, and we have the same authority to either accept or refuse. It will be a choice of one or the other. There is no middle ground.

Those in the kingdom of darkness take on the roles of priests. They do not live within the theocratic confines of the heavenly order of the theocratic monarchy.

They think adversely different. This beast is standing in a place in which it is not authorized to stand in.

It is a system of worship, where one believes that they can do anything they want in order to get into the presence of God. It's a kingdom that expresses itself with no power. It says it follows God but does not, because of the lack of belief in God within its citizens. This kingdom moulds its citizen's character as to however they themselves see fit. They believe they can do anything they want and still have God's approval. Their deeds are accompanied with signs but with lack of power. They are sick and sinful in their flesh. They offer sacrifices of what is pleasurable in their sight. Sacrifices or offerings given whether material or spiritual in the wrong spirit are considered an abomination before God.

They do things for God, instead of doing what He requires of them. God calls them to order, but they are deaf and cannot hear the Word of God who has the answers to their dilemmas.

They use constant conferences and prayer meetings without God telling them to do so, in order to bring power to an image that they alone have created. This image is created into something that doesn't closely resemble the Kingdom of God and His ways.

Where He wants submission, they are looking at how many offerings they can take up before God, so that He will show Himself.

Isaiah 1

13–17 "Quit your worship charades.

> I can't stand your trivial religious games:
> Monthly conferences, weekly Sabbaths, special meetings—
>> meetings, meetings, meetings—I can't stand one more!
>
> Meetings for this, meetings for that. I hate them!
>> You've worn me out!
>
> I'm sick of your religion, religion, religion,
>> while you go right on sinning.
>
> When you put on your next prayer-performance,
>> I'll be looking the other way.
>
> No matter how long or loud or often you pray,
>> I'll not be listening.
>
> And do you know why? Because you've been tearing
>> people to pieces, and your hands are bloody.
>
> Go home and wash up.
>> Clean up your act.
>
> Sweep your lives clean of your evildoings
>> so I don't have to look at them any longer.

This kingdom sets itself up apart from the Kingdom of God. They are constantly looking on what they can do in their lives to please God. They attend meetings and conferences constantly in order to be entertained, while the preachers themselves bring no change.

The people under the influence of this power keep hoping for something grand and miraculous. They also place their faith in those who have titles and not God appointed positions. They hope that man can give them the authority and power that only God has the ability to release.

Therefore they are left powerless and have no idea why. Under this influence the people are filled with lawlessness, greed and selfishness. Instead of being a city on a hill that emits the glory of God, it is an unfaithful city referred to as a whore and a harlot.

Isaiah
[21]How the faithful city
      has become a whore,

The faithful are a city on a hill that cannot be hidden. The unfaithful are a city is deemed a whore and a harlot. A harlot is one who commits adultery with someone other than her husband.

We are the church, the bride of Christ. When the bride wanders and is intimate with the ways of someone other than Christ, adultery is committed.

And you have polluted the land
>With your harlotries and your wickedness.
3 Therefore the showers have been withheld,
And there has been no latter rain.

You have had a harlot's forehead;
You refuse to be ashamed.

Without shame or reverential fear they go on in life as if nothing matters to God. When troubles arise they blame Him or curse Him for allowing such tribulation to hit their lives. They are self righteous and are unforgiving. They hold malice in their hearts, but yet will smile outwardly like a sly wolf waiting to pounce at first chance.

They believe their intellect and prayers are superior to any god that is out there, and they maintain their stance by praying longer and louder in effort to glorify themselves. They will study man made theology in order to gain their own personal degree of acceptance. They are usually terrified of dying and believe if they just say sorry with no intent, God will forgive them.

We are the church both individually and corporately. We are molded by who we allow to mold us. We are committed to who we believe is our husband. Our actions reflect our character. Those under this beast influence will concentrate on things and riches instead of the Gospel, the good news of the kingdom of God.

They preach get this in five ways or do these in ten ways. Their focus is on their problems and wants God to show up in their self made religion. They want Him to honor their prayers regardless of their honor to Him. They believe that praise and worship is some type of special dance or song to conjure up the spirit of God, when in reality they are conjuring up a spirit not of Him. Its disciples live toil filled lives, filled with frustration and oppression. Arrogance and a know it all attitude fills the pulpits and thus filters down to the congregants in the churches. Individuals in the churches therefore are without love for their fellow worshippers. Status and ego take over instead of lowliness and compassion. These are those who do not accept how God wishes for things to be done, but instead they replace His will with "my works doctrine." They take for granted the love of God, by disregarding what He wills for them in their lives. They will worship with all types of rituals, bowing down to statues that God never commanded anyone to do. They believe religion more than God, because they do not study under the direction of the Holy Spirit. They do not have a heavenly constitution, because where there is lawlessness, there is no law to uphold. They believe that the "law of grace" has them covered, in order to enable and allow them to participate in whatever behavior they desire. They take God for granted and do as they please. They believe that if they do wrong, that since God loves them, everything is alright to do.

Isaiah 2:6
> Philistine witchcraft, and pagan hocus-pocus,
> a world rolling in wealth,
>
> Stuffed with things,
> no end to its machines and gadgets,
> And gods—gods of all sorts and sizes.
> These people make their own gods and worship
> what they make.
>
> A degenerate race, facedown in the gutter.
> Don't bother with them! They're not worth forgiving![6]

These are those who have a casual acquaintance relationship with God. They call on Him only when they need Him, because then they see how powerless the god they are actually worshipping really is. When God gives them mercy, they repay Him with the same behavior He has just taken them out of. They are those who take the Word of God out of context, but believe they are teaching accurately the Word of God. These individuals either do not know or have not been taught the Good News of the Kingdom, the way that Jesus taught it. Either their leaders are keeping it for themselves or they have strayed away from the only thing Jesus told us to spread throughout the world. The Kingdom Gospel is to be the only way to make disciples, but instead they rely on their

---

[6] Peterson, E. H. (2002). *The Message: The Bible in contemporary language* (Is 2:6–9). Colorado Springs, Colo.: NavPress.

self made books and how to manuals to take people to a place that they themselves have never been.

Some will wear their long flowing robes and will be seating in places of honor in their communities, while their friends and followers are worshipping their image at their feet.

They have false christs or false anointed ones as well as false prophets in their midst, telling people want they want to hear. They are in all churches and all denominations. Their image is wealth and luxury with no troubles or trials. If this portrayal is not in the church corporately, it is in the church individually.

Lucifer was the most glorious and beautiful angel compared to all the other angels. He was filled with the joy of his own pride.

The Message | Is 13:19 And Babylon, most glorious of all kingdoms, the pride and joy of Chaldeans, Will end up smoking and stinking like Sodom, and, yes, like Gomorrah, when God had finished with them.

Those under the influence of this beast are adversarial to those who do not belong in their form of living. They block growth and advancement in others. They are opponents to royal policy and are rivals to anyone of the Kingdom of God. They are accusers. They are members of the heavenly court of God who wander about the earth, observing mankind and then wait to stand to accuse them. They appear to function as a servant, but gossip and backstab those to anyone who will listen.

Those in this kingdom have dual personalities and are either lukewarm or lackadaisical in the things of God.

People in this system are not open to or deny the personal revelatory process that God gives to His children. These are necessities for they are for the purposes of ruling in their predestined territory. Instead they take authority into areas they have not been given permission to overtake. They lack obedience and therefore lying and manipulation is an accepted form of behavior.

They make their own rules as they see fit and they use scripture to have it say what they want, instead of what God wants to reveal. There is no accountability enforced and an "untouchable" attitude is manifested. Their hypocritical minds will bend to popular opinion or the latest fad or trend that has captivated the world.

Their character is embedded in their minds and they handle their lives accordingly. Whatever they agree to becomes their covenant. They leave their mark by whatever they leave behind, whether it be pain, destruction or death. Satan's signature is on everything they do, because they have given their lives over to him because of what they believe.

They have exchanged or refused Christ's death on the cross, by not believing that how they worship God makes a difference. They do not believe they should suffer, because afterall that's what Jesus did.

They make excuses to stay the same, without providing reasons to change.

This kingdom is one with artificial light. It is a system of believing that the whole world stands at amazement at. They believe they are worshipping God, but really are worshipping a beast, one that appears to be like Him because of the easiness and charisma involved.

Individuals receive their power by what the beast is able to give them. What they believe is freedom is not really freedom at all. They ingest the lies of what the beast dictates, for they do not study to show themselves approved (right standing) by God. Instead they make their own "law of the land" which changes whenever circumstances change.

PROTOCOL TERMS FOR OPERATION IN THE KINGDOM OF DARKNESS

The kingdom of darkness operates in these terms in order to form an alliance against the Kingdom of God. He begins with injecting thoughts into the mind of the individual. Individuals must choose to accept these thoughts, actions and mindsets of non religious or religious beliefs. They do so by entertaining them and helping them flourish into other avenues. These ideas are non biblically based and function on an individual's past and present experiences. They cover all avenues of the individuals thought processes and are necessary for building his demonic alliance or covenant.

In this alliance, there is an exchange made between the person and demonic influential powers. This exchange is the opposite of Christ sacrifice on the cross.

Christ purchased us back and in thankfulness we honor Him. In the kingdom of darkness however, individuals sellout their inheritance for immediate gratification for ego centered reasons.

This operational alliance is based on buying and selling.

Satan offers the individual the terms that are usually based in self. When the individual believes in the term or terms, Satan has offered for spiritual purchase, the individual sells out in order to maintain the thought process. This buying and selling is the exchange that verifies the alliance and keeps one from entering the Kingdom of God.

Anyone who prefers this type of kingdom will unknowingly bow down to Satan with his terms, while simultaneously reject Christ's redemption for them. Once a person has entertained these terms and has clearly made a decision on which kingdom they will serve, they are marked in their hand or their foreheads.

These have not only validated who they identify with, but also they verify which kingdom they do not belong. Their character will be as those in the kingdom of darkness. It is written in their character and demonstrated in their actions, just as it is in the kingdom of God. Therefore they appear with the marked characteristics of whom they serve.

These are those who do not operate in where God has placed them. They are more concerned about their own lives that someone else. When someone tries to leave the kingdom of darkness, Satan sends fear to stop them operating in their sovereign power. He does not want these individuals to learn or know how much power they have, because if they would find out, the less influence over them he would have. He gains His power through strongholds of demonic influence. He knows his time is short and is at war with God and His Kingdom. His goal is to take over and kill as many as he can in order to prove himself in the heavenly courts.

When people accept the lies he tells them, they come into agreement and make an alliance to come against the kingdom of God.

- Must choose to accept that God loves you, so you can do what you want.
- Must choose to accept that God wants people to be poor and sick
- Must choose to accept God doesn't kill people
- Must choose to accept that since you love God, you will have no problems

- Must choose to accept that you just have to be a good person to go to heaven or operate in the kingdom of God
- Must choose to accept that God doesn't love bad people
- Must choose to accept God only loves certain denominations
- Must choose to accept God gives you brownie points for all the good deeds that you do
- Must choose to accept God knows that your religion is better than others because....
- Must choose to accept God doesn't want you to wear jewelry or makeup
- Must choose to accept God only wants preachers to preach the gospel
- Must choose to accept God cares about titles in the church
- Must choose to accept that God thinks you're evil since you do bad things
- Must choose to accept God is not stronger than the devil
- Must choose to accept that how you see God overrides how others see Him
- Must choose to accept God doesn't love you because....
- Must choose to accept If you're a good person you will enter the kingdom of God
- Must choose to accept The kingdom of God and heaven are the same thing
- Must choose to accept that as long as I go to church on Sunday and on important days, that's all God wants
- Must choose to accept God loves some people more than others
- Must choose to accept Bad things only happen to bad

people

- Must choose to accept that when bad things happen to you that means you're evil and deserve it
- Must choose to accept that all preachers go to heaven
- Must choose to accept the rock that Jesus spoke about to Peter is the catholic church
- Must choose to accept that preachers are all holy
- Must choose to accept that you don't have to read your bible because that's what preachers are for
- Must choose to accept that you are not able to understand the bible, its only for clergy to know
- Must choose to accept the end of the world is on a certain date and time
- Must choose to accept you can do what you want and still be in kingdom of God ways
- Must choose to accept God doesn't discipline
- Must choose to accept God is not interested in your everyday affairs
- Must choose to accept God is only for Sunday and you can do what you want during the week
- Must choose to accept God wants you to suffer because you deserve it
- Must choose to accept God only wants your good deeds
- Must choose to accept God just sits up in the sky waiting to beat you over the head when you do something wrong
- Must choose to accept that since you go to church

every week you are more holy than someone who doesn't
- Must choose to accept the church is only a building

- Must choose to accept if you have done something wrong, you have to have penance for the rest of your life
- Must choose to accept The only way to confess your sin is to tell it to a priest
- Must choose to accept If a preacher has taken part of a sin, we should disown and disassociate with him or her for the rest of his or her life
- Must choose to accept All preachers that preach on television are fake
- Must choose to accept God only does things in ways that make sense
- Must choose to accept God hates homosexuals
- Must choose to accept God cares about how much money you put in the offering
- Must choose to accept God is like a vending machine; you put money in and out comes what you want
- Must choose to accept that you must have a degree in order to preach the gospel
- Must choose to accept good people have no enemies
- Must choose to accept God doesn't care what you do during the week, as long as you go to church on Sunday
- Must choose to accept If you say a prayer for God to forgive you before I do something unrighteous, you're okay
- Must choose to accept you don't believe in God, therefore He doesn't exist
- Must choose to accept as long as you say "I'm saved}, I'm saved!
- Must choose to accept God doesn't care about how you treat others, just as long as you treat Him good.

- Must choose to accept God will never allow sickness in people who are good
- Must choose to accept other peoples prayers are stronger than your own
- Must choose to accept God is not to be talked about, He is only to be mentioned in church
- Must choose to accept God only likes certain types of music
- Must choose to accept that if you have a title in church you are extra special and anointed
- Must choose to accept God doesn't talk to people, He only talks to preachers
- Must choose to accept The Glory of God only hits those who "fall out"
- Must choose to accept If you look spiritual therefore you are spiritual
- Must choose to accept God is not interested in your life in your home, only your life when you are in church
- Must choose to accept God doesn't love mega churches
- Must choose to accept If God loved you, you wouldn't be going through this
- Must choose to accept that you are baptized if you had water poured over your head
- Must choose to accept Eve ate an apple in the garden
- Must choose to accept you can never do what Jesus did.
- Must choose to accept the holier you are, the bigger the church you have.
- Must choose to accept Heaven is full of harps and puffy clouds

- Must choose to accept that you can do what you want and God will understand
- Must choose to accept If you don't like a certain preacher, he must not be from God
- Must choose to accept miracles are not real, there are reasons for everything
- Must choose to accept you don't have to do anything to make your life better, because this is what God wants
- Must choose to accept that you don't have to work, God will take care of your bills
- Must choose to accept you only need to talk to God when you're in trouble or when you need something
- Must choose to accept that If God doesn't do what you want Him to do, then He doesn't love you
- Must choose to accept God can only do certain things on certain days
- Must choose to accept God doesn't interrupt people's lives
- Must choose to accept It must not be God, because He isn't answering the prayer like you want Him to.
- Must choose to accept God doesn't hear you
- Must choose to accept God likes it when you impose self inflicted suffering in order to pay for your sins and get His approval
- Must choose to accept God can't use you because you have made too many mistakes in your life
- Must choose to accept Jesus last name is Christ
- Must choose to accept God just wants you to be a good person and that's it

- Must choose to accept God doesn't want a relationship with you
- Must choose to accept there is no hell
- Must choose to accept Jesus was just a good man on the earth
- Must choose to accept the bible doesn't apply any longer
- Must choose to accept If you get divorced you are not going to heaven
- Must choose to accept babies who are not baptized don't go to heaven
- Must choose to accept your dead relatives answer your prayers
- Must choose to accept there are many ways to the Father
- Must choose to accept there are no prophets in this day and age
- Must choose to accept since you have gone to church all your life, you know who God is
- Must choose to accept If you read the bible from one to many times, you know all what God has to say
- Must choose to accept God is only concerned if you read the bible
- Must choose to accept as long as you say the right prayers, sing the right song, give the right money, I'm definitely holy in God's eyes
- Must choose to accept your good deeds and fulfilling of sacraments is a guarantee you're going to heaven
- Must choose to accept IF you feel good coming out of church then God is happy with you
- Must choose to accept God already knows what's going to

happen in your life, so it doesn't really matter what you do.
- Must choose to refuse the Cross of Salvation in any or all ways

In Conclusion

See things from His perspective and when you do, your old life is dead. Your new life, which is your real Life even though invisible to spectators—is with Christ in God. He is your life. When Christ (your real life, remember) shows up again on this earth, you'll show up, too—the real you, the glorious you. Meanwhile, be content with obscurity like Christ.

And that means killing off everything connected with that way of death: sexual promiscuity, impurity, lust, doing whatever you feel like whenever you feel like it, and grabbing whatever attracts your fancy. That's a life shaped by things and feelings instead of by God. It's because of this kind of thing that God is about to explode in anger. It wasn't long ago that you were doing all that stuff and not knowing any better. But you know better now, so make sure it's all gone for good: bad temper, irritability, meanness, profanity, dirty talk.

Don't lie to one another. You're done with that old life. It's like a filthy set of ill-fitting clothes you've stripped off and put in the fire. Now you're dressed in a new wardrobe.

Every item of your new way of life is custom-made by the Creator, with his label on it. All the old fashions are now obsolete. Words like Jewish and non-Jewish, religious and irreligious, insider and outsider, uncivilized and uncouth, slave and free, mean nothing.

From now on everyone is defined by Christ, everyone is included in Christ.

So, chosen by God for this new life of love, dress in the wardrobe God picked out for you: compassion, kindness, humility, quiet strength, discipline. Be even-tempered, content with second place, quick to forgive an offense. Forgive as quickly and completely as the Master forgave you. And regardless of what else you put on, wear love. It's your basic, all-purpose garment. Never be without it.

Let the peace of Christ keep you in tune with each other, in step with each other. None of this going off and doing your own thing. And cultivate thankfulness. Let the Word of Christ—the Message—have the run of the house. Give it plenty of room in your lives.

Instruct and direct one another using good common sense. And sing, sing your hearts out to God! Let every detail in your lives—words, actions, whatever—be done in the name of the Master, Jesus, thanking God the Father every step of the way.

The thing that separates God's system from the World's system is character. It is the determining factor that God takes the final issue with. Those in this system see God as an extension of themselves instead of seeing God as He is; high and lifted up.

He wants us to choose the kingdom of which one we want to be a citizen.

Choose whom you will serve.

The Last Word

A Letter To My People

My Dearest Children,

I AM A God of order and structure. I AM always in the process of building you up to for My glory. You were made in Our likeness. The combination that I use to propel you to make choices.

Each choice in your life is a test of perpetual faith, that enables you to walk in a higher level of authority. You must learn rule and operate in this kingly authority so that you will be able to experience My power within you.

Do not worry about making a mistake when you reach any decision. When you believe in Me and walk in the boundaries that are from Me, then trust I AM protecting you.
Listen to MY voice. My Word is My Voice. If you listen to anything besides My Word, then who are you listening to?

My Word does not entice. My Word brings peace. My Word does not tickle your ears; it gives you wisdom to enable you to rise above. My Word does not bring you trouble; it brings you THROUGH trouble.

I speak clearly. You innately know right from wrong, good and evil. I speak in a language that you clearly understand. I do not bring confusion, for I AM not the author of it.

I AM a God of Order. I created Adam first, then Eve. I gave Adam (man) instructions not eat of the Tree of Knowledge of Good and Evil. Adam was to rule in that instruction and be a demonstration to his wife. He was placed in a position of authority.

Just as I covered Adam, he was to cover Eve with his life which came from My life.

Many believe that they were disobedient when they had come into contact with the serpent. But I Am your God. I Am Sovereign. There is nothing that I do not know. Man does not realize that for them to encounter the serpent, they were led to be tempted by him. They were led there to be tempted in the same way that My Son Jesus was tempted in the wilderness.

As with any soldier in My heavenly army, your faith must be strengthened. Without strengthening you will not be able to withstand evil and guard against it.

This strengthening allows you to come into alignment with My Word so that you will be matured and be held blameless because I know you withstood with strength of character and integrity.

When Eve ate the fruit, she was uncovered by the man that I appointed to watch over her. I placed Adam in appointed position with personal responsibility. He was not to be the boss of her and control her; he was created to be the head of her and to lead her. He was to maintain the authority that I gave him, so that they would both stay aligned with My will.

However they did not heed my Word.

Not being in alignment with My instructions, they crossed the boundary that I had placed around them for their protection. Not heeding My Word they created a detoured path that led them away from My refuge.

Misalignment caused unnecessary conversations from an enemy who didn't want them to succeed. It also caused accusations in the heavenly courts from those who wanted to overthrow My seat of power. This pathway caused a demonic agenda to activate.

Some have stated that this was a test of obedience, but moreover this was a test of faith.

It was a test of their trust in Me.

. I AM God. Be assured that there is nothing that I do not know. There is nothing new under the sun and there is nothing that is that wasn't with me before it was.

I AM wisdom. Wisdom comes from Me. I AM The Word for the every word that I speak must manifest. I will make certain that My Word comes forth filled and not void or empty. I make certain that nothing can come up against My Word, for it is true and sharper than a two edged sword. In comfort you should know that nothing will interfere in my plans for you, if you believe in Me.

Yes, if you believe in My Word.

I have established boundaries to separate what is of Me and what is not. Adam and Eve are an example of what happens when you separate your love from Me. This separation comes when you are in rebellion to My plans for you ,as it connects to the purpose you were created.

Your identity is in Me.
Your identity is connected to Me.

I created you, therefore I know whom I have made you to be.

The world has taught you confusion and your churches have taught you greed. You have been taught to not suffer and that you should always be poor and in need.

You do not realize who you are when you ask of Me, and when you speak to Me.

I know how you believe in Me by the way you present your Spirit in My Presence.

I compare our visits to that of being invited to a dinner. When you sit down and eat in the presence of a king but you only give attention to the food at the table. When you take no regard to who is feeding you, then you exalt yourself in My presence.

Your perception is not focused. You are not seeing who I really Am. It has been clouded by preacher magicians, sorcery and manipulation from earthly pulpits. I remember Adam was looking at being a steward of a garden, while I was training Him in the operation of ruler ship over an earthly domain.

You receive My Word in the right context, but issued with the wrong motives. You receive tidbits of information and draw complete conclusions. You put faith more in people than you do in Me. You look for sin, when sin is everywhere and in everyone. You are looking for reasons for downfalls in others, when you should be looking on what I AM actually doing in you.

So I will teach you as I did with Adam and Eve on how to live a disciplined life. I will bring you revelation to transform your mind. I have not escaped accusations and trouble and neither will you.

You need to know this. Some of you have been taught that you will not suffer if you love Me. Some of you have learned that bad things happen to you, when you do something bad. While the latter may be true you must acknowledge that you will have trials and tribulation in this life. They are the testing grounds in which decisions have the opportunity to be integrated into building your spiritual character.

Trials are necessary to strengthen your three stranded cord to me and are necessary to further entrench the boundaries established in your life.

You are no different from Adam and Eve as far as My wishes and heartfelt desires are for you. I was training them as to how powerful their minds were; but they gave themselves over to doubt because of their disbelief. They took me for granted and pride caused them to give themselves over to an adversary that appeared harmless.

My perspective of mankind is different from man. I saw and created mankind as rulers over every living thing. I created you to rule over the creatures, which includes serpents. I created you to rule over your animalistic desires. I created you to rule over every living thing, for just as Adam and Eve there is "life" in your name, just as there is life in Me.

Your ruler ship which embodies authority is always subject to Me. I gave Adam and Eve, your first earthly parents to rule over the earth, its matters, but not become part of it.

Regardless of what anyone says or does, or what circumstances that may or may not appear, My Word is strong. It is the foundation that you must stand on in order to stay in alignment and obedience to My Word.

This foundation is so strong that Satan's followers are not able to stand upon it. His name is the "prince of power of the air." Air has no foundation. It has no basis to build on.

I Am the light that guides your pathway. Satan is not light. He was stripped of His title Lucifer. Before he was light, now he only appears as light. He cannot rule in my atmosphere. His words can only speak against it.

When Satan speaks he manifests a twisting of truth. His aim is to attack your kingship with doubt, so that you will question who you are. He does this to lure you out of your position and My established boundaries. He knows that within the boundaries I set forth there is safety.

Satan's word travels and creates its own energy through non tangible effects of emotion and logic. He uses the airwaves to impress and express his thoughts and ideas into your mind, to gain access into the Kingdom of God which is in you. The Kingdom of God is my operational way of doing things. They are My ways and they can be learned if you wish to intimately partake of them. They are in your mind. This is why Satan will always attack your mind through your integrity and your character.

He knows that once he can speak to your mind and have you appeal to his thoughts and ideas, then he is able to take you away from My Presence and bring you into his.

I want you to come back to your position. I want you back in righteousness which is your right standing with Me. I want you in alignment with Me.

My Word is sure. I want to cloak you with righteousness. I Am not your enemy. I do not accuse you. I cover you and I have got you covered if you will accept my sacrifice.

Satan has no covering no robe of righteousness from Me. He wants your covering so that you will embody his traits, character and mindset.

You give away your covering when you go outside the boundaries I have established. When Adam and Eve left My presence in their time of testing, their covering simultaneously came off when they turned to the power of the serpent.

Satan had them thinking on his level. When I ask you to repent, I ask you to turn away from that way of thinking.

When you interact and entertain him on his level, you expose yourself to Me in nakedness.

When you share in Satan's mind and you believe his news, you don't feel a need for covering because he is filled with an artificial light.

When you are without covering in My Presence, you cannot help but feel ashamed, for I Am the only One that can give true light.

When you come to Me in shame, do not confuse it with guilt. Shame allows Me to clothe you, but guilt allows you to believe you are condemned for the rest of your life.

It is My life and the light of My Son which covers you. Anything else is a deception, because nothing is hidden from Me.

My glory surrounded them and I clothed them initially with the radiance and love that is Me. There is a certain glory that is manifested in My Presence. It has the ability to clothe and comfort. It leads and satisfies you like nothing other. It manifests itself when there is no relational separation between you and I.

I Am love and mercy. I wasn't trying to be cruel in the garden. Adam and Eve were simply in training. You are to learn from what they missed. I AM your Father, Your King. Come to me and I will give you rest.

Peace Be With You

Scriptures taken from the Holy Bible

Books

Genesis,

Kings

Isaiah

Mathew

Mark

Luke

John

Peter

Acts

James

Revelation

For more information on the Kingdom of God or to order additional copies of this material please visit www.kingdomgov.com

Or www.kingdomconstitution.com For media inquiries please email Prophetic Media Group media@kingdomgov.com

www.ingramcontent.com/pod-product-compliance
Lightning Source LLC
Chambersburg PA
CBHW070637160426
43194CB00009B/1487